How I becam[e]

DANCING QU[...]
PALM SPRI[...]

A memoire of Body, Mind & Spirit
Transformation

JILL ANN LANGHAM

DEDICATION & THANKS

This book is dedicated to a number of people who have helped me along the way. First of all, I dedicate this book to my parents, Alma & Guido Bianchi, for without you I would not be here at all. Thank you both for providing me with the tools to make the most out of your best attributes. I love you.

Next, I want to thank Steve Langham, Sameer Ismail, Eric Vander Linden, Robby Sherwin and Bill Sinunu, for assisting me in getting my message out and without who's help this book could not have been started or finished! Thank you from the bottom of my heart!

I also want to express my gratitude to Luis Gavela, Vincent Corrales and Claus Kjolsen for helping me present the Best Version of Me! You are all incredibly talented!

There are of course a myriad of people throughout my life who have guided and influenced me, but I've chosen to acknowledge the people who helped me with this particular project. I trust that those other people will know who I mean and will accept this more generic "thank you" from me to you!

And lastly, I dedicate this book to the entire Gay Community. You are the first community who accepted me for being exactly who I was meant to be. Your love, support and encouragement have allowed me to soar, and spread my wings and my love. You have brought me *to* life, and I will forever be your biggest cheerleader and your **Dancing Queen**!

THANK YOU, ONE AND ALL! XOXO

PROLOGUE

Many of the events that took place in my life have not only a rhyme and reason but often a pattern as well. Most of us seem to see our lives changing year to year but after writing about my life, I began to see these patterns in a more linear way. I found patterns associated with holidays, anniversaries, seasons, and more.

While the chronology of each chapter is not always linear or even exact, by the end, you will see what I have come to know; that our lives, and mine in particular, are lived within the confines of the calendar to a great extent. In this book, I have chosen to segment them into months of the year since one of the primary lessons they have shown me is that certain things, both good and bad, seem to repeat themselves during certain months over many years.

I now see so many of these patterns more clearly and understand much better the choices that I have made, both good and sometimes harmful. I have been consciously choosing to leave my more dramatic self on the dance floor rather than in my every day life and it has proven to be a wise decision for me.

While writing about my memories, I am sharing the stories of those with whom these memories were made. It is not my place to discuss their issues but yet I do need to share some of who they are and were in order to elucidate the effect that they had on me. I have tried to be as gentle as I could with the times that we shared and I hope that I have been fair and honest.

I believe that there are no accidents in life. The partners and friends that I have chosen, the work, the cities in which I have lived, the decisions I have made, were all done in an attempt to teach myself the lessons I needed to learn in order to grow and evolve. I'd like to believe that these same friends, partners, and places chose me for the same reasons, whether they are aware of it or not.

I have so much more love in my life and so many people who really care that it brings a great joy to me, a joy I feel even as I write this.

In a million years I could not have predicted that I would become the **Dancing Queen of Palm Springs**. I could never have foreseen my growth and evolution into someone who the Gay Community would come to love and respect. I did not know that I had so much in common with gay men, yet I do. It still amazes me that it is through my Dancing that we have all come together. It is my hope that by reading about my journey, you may gain some insights into your own lives and perhaps recognize some of your own patterns as well.

FEBRUARY

FEBRUARY 1974

In February 1974 I was in my first year of Nursing School at Buffalo General School of Nursing in New York. Besides taking classes at the school itself, we also attended classes at the University of Buffalo. It is there that I met my second long term boyfriend, Rob a handsome, well built, Polish guy (what is it with me and Poland?) Ironically, his Dad knew my mother from high school making his Dad a fan of mine but his mother, not so much!

We met on campus and immediately started dating. I should mention that this was a pattern of mine and as a matter of fact I didn't know any other way to be. If I met a guy and we liked one another, we would go on one date and instantly start a relationship. I have really only dated a few people in my life but have had quite a few relationships. I think this is why at 62 years of age I don't know how to date because I've never really done it before. And this time was no different.

Polish Rob and I were going strong and had just gotten through Christmas and New Year's with Valentine's Day approaching fast. We used to smoke a lot of pot together and would dive headfirst into the munchies. We used to eat lots of ice cream in those days and it helped that his best friend, Jimmy, worked for an ice cream store. With Jimmy's help, we would break into the shop after hours and raid the freezers. We'd take the huge tubs of ice cream out of the freezer and would eat them half-way down before returning them to the ice cream cases. I'll bet you're going to think about this the next time you get ice cream scooped from a large tub at an ice cream store! Sorry about that.

It was a rainy afternoon the first time I dropped acid with Rob and Jimmy, the ice cream supplier. Our plan was to go shopping at the mall then go to the movies to see the Disney Classic, Fantasia, and then end up raiding the ice cream store.

The boys picked me up at my dorm and Rob handed me a tiny piece of blotter paper, which held the acid, and told me to hold it under my tongue till it disintegrated, which I did. We then drove to the mall to buy one another's Valentine's Day presents.

I had been working two jobs while going to school full time and had set aside $80 for his gift. This was a lot of money in those days and I had been looking to buy him a blue sapphire ring to match his big, blue eyes. I knew exactly where I was going in the mall and headed straight to Zale's on my own. I went inside and began perusing the cases until I found the rings I was looking for. I asked the salesman to show me a few, which he did. I chose one that was about $72 so with tax it would come in just under the $80 that I had allotted.

As he was showing me the ring, I noticed that my vision seemed to change and I thought something really odd was going on. At first I thought I was getting sick until I realized I was starting to feel the acid coming on. By the time the salesman came back with the bill and told me how much I owed I was totally tripping!

For the life of me I could not figure out how to pay the bill with the four $20 bills that I had in my hand because the amount was $74.16 and I could not understand the $4.16 part! It was quite funny actually and after stressing out completely, I just handed him the four $20's and told him to take what he needed. I headed back to the car, gift in tow, high as a kite.

The rest of the day and night were nothing but fun! No bad trips for this girl. We had a blast, watching Fantasia. It is still one of my very favorite Disney movies. The three of us partied, ate tons of ice cream and sat in the car during a rainstorm watching the raindrops hit the windshield, making interesting designs as they ran down the glass. Tripping on acid, I saw things that I am certain would have made a very interesting Rorschach test! I gave Rob the ring on Valentine's Day, which he loved but, as life happens, we broke up three months later.

It's been years since Valentine's Day was anything more than just another day of another year. I hate how commercial we have become and that very few holidays hold any special meaning for me. Still, there is something to be said for the first Valentines Day with that special somebody. I am truly a romantic at heart. But not all Valentine's Day are created equal.

A case in point: another Valentine's Day Massacre.

Robert was a ballet dancer and a true athlete. While being a totally unique character, he was also diagnosed with Borderline Personality Disorder. I had never been with any one who had that diagnosis before and let me just mention that, at best, it is a very difficult experience.

He was very secretive and paranoid, but I didn't realize or appreciate it at the time. He told me his name was Robert when he called me on the phone to ask me out. He had gotten my name from a mutual friend. I was intrigued by his voice, and thrilled when he asked if I liked to dance. I happened to mention that as much as I loved to dance, I was no Baryshnikov. This was odd because I had never used that expression before. After we had a laugh about this coincidence, we talked about his ballet experience and it had an obvious effect on me, and my judgment of him early on. I had always wanted to be a dancer but knew I didn't have the body type they were looking for so it remained a pipe dream.

As I have alluded to before with my history of dating, Robert and I had one date and immediately began a relationship. He was very different from anyone that I had ever been with. I had been in a treatment program previously and had chosen to be drug and alcohol free. Ironically, now we were both drug and alcohol free so we used sex as our drug. We were incredibly compatible and both loved having tons of sex. We would lay in bed for hours, having one orgasm after another until we were exhausted. We spent a lot of time together and when we got along, it was great. Yet, when intimacy became to constricting and his disorder flared up he would push me far away. I had a co-dependent personality myself but also didn't know what that really meant in terms of my own behavior. I just know that I was hurt by his distancing behavior but also just addicted enough to put up with it. My theme, my problem, his actions only compounded it.

I was always on pins and needles around him and was never really sure exactly where I stood. This was a very familiar feeling to me, reminding me of my childhood home. I was so painfully insecure that I'm certain that I would have put up with anything in order to have a connection with this man. This, again, was MY pattern and this time with this man was no different!

It was only by accident that I found out that he had lied about his name. One day, as I was getting into his car, I had to move the mail that was sitting on the passenger seat. Rather than sitting on it, I picked it up and put it on my lap, which made sense to me at the time.

I glanced down at the envelopes only to see a name I didn't recognize. I asked him if he was picking up his neighbors mail to which he quickly answered; "No, it's mine!" He shot me a look that signaled, instantly, that this was not all right. He became highly agitated, appeared very threatened and angry, and told me to mind my own business as he ripped the mail out of my hands and threw it into the back seat. I flashed back on feeling guilty as a child and like the bad girl I always thought I was.

He was also a very disciplined man, a fanatic about the way he ate, and totally obsessive compulsive in all aspects of his nature. He was the first person that told me about being a vegan. He explained the principles and benefits of dry skin brushing my body and he convinced me eat to organic foods. Because of this regimen, I lost about eight pounds and felt really great. He taught me a lot in the six to eight months that we dated but it was this particular Valentine's Day that sticks out in my mind years later.
Robert was a jazz fan and collected every recording of Frank Sinatra's that had ever been made. I was a huge Sinatra fan myself and had never before met a person like Robert. He had thousands of hours of Sinatra recorded and would make me the most amazing mixed tapes. I decided to surprise him for our Valentine's Day so I planned to dress up as Sinatra himself and lip synch one of our favorite songs and then serve him a delicious, organic, vegan meal.

I set up the dining room table as I imagined it would look in Las Vegas. I had special lighting to set the mood and a sign on my front door that said "Please Enter". As soon as he opened the door, I started the music and stood there waiting for him to round the corner. I was wearing a tailored man's suit with a white raincoat slung over my shoulder. I tipped a Fedora jauntily off my head, partially covering my face and I began to lip synch the Sinatra classic.

I performed the whole number while he stood there grinning from ear to ear! It was truly a great moment and we were both totally in the mood. I greeted him with a pretend cocktail since we were both clean and sober and then ushered him to his seat where I began to serve him dinner. I had made a scroll for the menu out of parchment paper, writing the menu in gold leaf pen and had it rolled up using thin gold rope. It was all going so well.

We sat down and I served the first course; an organic salad made with fresh greens, mushrooms, tomatoes, and cucumbers and dressed with garlic and olive oil with fresh sea salt and pepper. We were both in such great moods. Sinatra continued to serenade us while we ate. We were almost done with the salads when Robert asked where I had managed to find the organic tomatoes as he had been to all the co-ops around town and couldn't find any.

I immediately felt my stomach drop. I felt nervous and scared to answer. I already knew that Robert was a stickler for everything organic. I wanted to fib and say that I gotten them at a different co-op but I wasn't a good liar so I confessed that although everything else in the salad was organic, the tomatoes were not. He immediately threw down his fork and said, "You're feeding me something that is not organic, how dare you?" I was flabbergasted; he had to be kidding, right?

But, no, he was not.

He shoved his chair back, stood up and said, "I'm leaving!" "What?" was all I managed to squeak out! "No, you can't! I've spent all day making all of your favorite foods."

His ears were deaf to my comments. He was done and that was it! No amount of reasoning was going to matter to him. I felt this instantly, in the pit of my stomach. He stormed out, refusing to talk to me or even look at me.

I was totally devastated. I was in shock. I was hurt and angry but also afraid of being alone. I tried to call him for the rest of the evening but always got his answering machine. The one time he actually did pick up the phone he slammed the receiver down as soon as he heard my voice. I was so insecure at that point in time that it hurts my soul to think about it now. I had no self-love; in fact I had no relationship with myself whatsoever.

I would have rather been with him then to be alone!

I think he punished me for almost ten days by not returning any of my phone calls before finally calling me back. He acted as if nothing had happened and asked if I wanted to get together. I'm sad to say that I really needed to choose him rather than honoring my self and my soul. My choice was already made.

This was a first hand look at personality disorders and should have been my wake-up call but I dove back in, again. I was addicted to rejection and he was the perfect person to be rejected by. We did this dance for another two months before finally going our separate ways at the end of April. I was hurt and felt rejected but also felt a huge sense of relief.

MARCH

MARCH 1991

My house was broken into in September of 1990 while I was living in downtown Albuquerque, N.M. It wasn't until March of 1991 that I finally got the reimbursement check from my insurance company for the stolen goods. I was excited because I would now finally have the money to buy a coach ticket to fly to Europe, a place I had been trying to get to since I was 17 years old.

Somewhere deep in the recesses of my brain, I've always felt a connection to Europe but strangely not to Italy, where my Dad's family was originally from. Instead, I was pulled towards England. I have fantasized many times that I would marry a Brit, their sexy accents are a turn-on!

In 1973, I'd prayed that I could go to Europe as part of my graduation gift from High School but my plans changed when I realized that I could graduate in 1972 as a junior and be done with the travesties of high school. I never took that trip, instead it would be 19 years later and a lot can change in 19 years.

So it came that in mid-March 1991, I boarded a plane in Albuquerque and made my way across the Atlantic. I awoke as we were approaching Munich, Germany. Even from the air I could see the difference in humidity, density, and architecture! I loved it. I was heading to Italy to visit my Dad's side of the family and his history, as much as I could discover.

Once on the ground, I found my way to my hotel. I had been instructed by some seasoned travelers to fight the urge to go to right to sleep but to only succumb after 6pm in order to combat the dreaded jetlag. Heeding their sage advice, I changed into my running clothes and jogged around the city, attempting to familiarize myself with it so that I could navigate it better after a refreshing shower. As coincidence would have it, President Mikhail Gorbachev was in town and was walking down the street with his security team. I stopped my run to watch him pass, seeing the wine-stain birthmark on his forehead as clear as day. It was very international and very exciting for this virgin traveler!

I was very shy when on my own back then and so, at this time and place, I kept to myself. I avoided strangers, especially since the German accent was one that was hard on my ears and the fact that I maybe knew two words in German. I felt very alone. I ate at a table for one and mostly walked the streets taking in the architecture and design marvels that this brilliant culture had produced over the centuries.

I spent only one night there before catching the overnight train to Verona, Italy where I would transfer through Venice and head to my final destination of Udine, in the Friuli region of Italy. This was the home of my 2nd cousins. I remember how frightened I was of getting robbed on the train. I was nervous all through the night and clutched my money under my makeshift pillow! When we crossed the border from Germany into Italy, soldiers boarded the train to check our passports while the conductors came through the train to check our tickets. It was all very disruptive, foreign, and excitingly part of the adventure.

My Dad had contacted his cousins to tell them that I was on my way. I had never met these cousins before and of course was anxious. My Dad suggested that I should tell them what I would be wearing so he could pass it on to them. I wore a mid-calf length canary yellow wool coat, leather pants, and cowboy boots to stand out (always a fashion statement)!

Sure enough, my relatives quickly picked me out at the train station as I disembarked later that day. I will never forget the looks on their faces when they recognized me. They were so welcoming; hugging and kissing me while grabbing my bags and whisking me off in their car and on to their century-old, newly remodeled, family home!

In two weeks time, these unknown relatives became my favorite people in the world. My older cousin was conversant in English, making it a bit easier to communicate. I carried my translation book with me 24/7. It was fascinating how much my brain worked on that trip. I actually went to bed with a sore head. The fascinating part of this experience is how much we actually learned about one another. When I was attempting to communicate with my relatives, I didn't want to miss one word. I found myself listening to every word and then would attempt to choose my responses very carefully because I really wanted to be heard and understood.

This was an entirely new experience for me because I was "unheard" in my family back home and carried an inadequacy into my everyday life even after moving out of the family home. I always knew I had something important to say but had been conditioned to be "silent", always stuffing down my feelings with food. The difference on this trip is that my cousins were open to my ways and me. They allowed me to speak up for myself. This was a uniquely new experience and a refreshing change in my life. They were also so generous with me that I was spoiled by the attention and the gifts that they continually showered upon me.

It was an amazing trip in so many ways. The first week, I traveled with my "fluent cousin" as he had taken off work from the railroad to show his American cousin around. Who does that? Not the Americans I knew! He took another cousin and me to Venice, Trieste, and to what used to be Yugoslavia just so I could get my passport stamped from yet another exotic country!

The next week, my other cousin took off a week from the Post Office to show me my grandmother Nonni's hometown of Codroipo, about thirty minutes from Udine. The current population of Codroipo is almost 15,000 but I was told that back at the turn of the 20th century there were only a few hundred people living there. Amazingly, the house that my Nonni lived in way back then was still standing! It was quite fascinating to see. The sense of family history and continuity were both new and fascinating to me.

We had been led to believe that both of my grandparents were from Codroipo but my new-found cousins relayed a very different version of this story.

According to them, my grandfather was from Florence. Evidently he got into some type of trouble there and whether he was fleeing arrest, or the fist, or the gun barrel of a girl's father that he had gotten pregnant, I will never know. Regardless, his punishment was to be sent to his relative's house in Codroipo where he met and wooed my grandmother.

The next week I left Udine to travel on my own, making my way to both Milan and Florence. I did not really enjoy Milan even though it was very much like Chicago. I found it to be cold and unfriendly. I saw some beautiful architecture there but felt no connection. I stayed at the youth hostile, sharing a room with two other young girls but I remained mostly isolated again, due to my creeping insecurities.

Florence, on the other hand, was magnificent to me! Was it because I now knew that part of me hailed from here? I will never know. I just knew that I loved everything about it and to this day have a love affair with this city. I ate, I shopped, I went to the museums and churches; and I dreamed. It was as if for the first time in my life, I was feeling my Italian roots. Florence really felt like a home-place and its beauty, grace, history, art, and the majesty of its ancient architecture mesmerized me.

Years later, in 1999, I met my parents in Italy for my Dad's 75th birthday and I took them on their first trip to Florence. We were staying in a Pensione overlooking the main Piazza, the central gathering spot for all people, Florentine and foreigners alike. The first morning as we perused the nearby scenery, my Dad spotted a sign for a bicycle shop. The sign gave the owner's name, Guido Bianchi. This just so happens to be my father's name! We were overjoyed and, after waiting around for the shop to open, ventured in to meet the owner. He got such a thrill out of my parents Friulian accent as well as being his "namesake". My Dad actually reinforced the coincidence by showing him his New York State driver's license.

My Nonni had been the one who told us about her roots and her story was that our grandfather was from Codroipo. She was a very strong-willed woman that you did not want to cross. As a result, I never shared the story about my grandfather actually being from Florence and did not suggest to my Dad that this bike shop owner could actually be a long lost relative. Sometimes, history is best left up to the ages and not a thing to be casually tampered with.

Over time, I have come up with my own version of the story about my grandfather. My fantasy-theory is that he got my grandmother pregnant and the two of them were exiled from both their town and the country. I say this because my grandmother came to America through Ellis Island at the age of 16 and did not return to Italy till the 1950's. My grandfather died at the young age of 42 of a heart attack leaving my grandmother as a fairly young widow in their newly adopted country.

By the time she took her first trip back, her parents were already dead and I think that is part of the reason she waited so long to return. I believe she wasn't welcome or at least felt that way. Although travel in those days was expensive, it wasn't a matter of money because, shockingly, my grandmother had done well buying and operating a bar! She and my godfather, Aldo, had a band together and entertained their guests at the bar. My grandmother was a singer-entertainer and my godfather a bass player! Kind of fits doesn't it? Maybe, it's my time to open a bar and club!

March 1996

It's funny but if you had known me back then, I dressed a lot like Laura Ingalls Wilder from Little House on the Prairie with my long skirts and cowboy boots. My body was always covered except my arms, which to this day, I always think look fat! The length of the dresses also hid my saddlebags.

Back in those days, I was running at least 5 days a week, 5 miles a day, and working out but my body rigidly hung onto the excess fat in those areas. I would cut my calories more and more and then would binge due to starvation. As a result my body shape would never really budge and all the muscles that I had were covered in what I viewed as a fat suit. I never weighed more than 127 pounds but due to inflammation, my body looked much larger than it really was. I was constantly frustrated trying to become the ideal me that was in my mind.

I remember when men and women used to play the guessing game of "how much do you think she weighs?" Inevitably, I'd be with one of my friends who was close to my size and build. The guy would always say I weighed 20 pounds more than I did and that my friend weighed 20 pounds less! It drove me crazy!

I co-owned a folk arts store with my then boyfriend, Matt. While he was on a buying trip to Poland in March of 1996 for our store in Santa Fe, I decided to have my first liposuction procedure. My workout partner at the time had a daughter who was a secretary in a plastic surgeon's office and could get me a cash discount, which brought it within my limited budget.

I was running the store on my own and was able to have our one and only part-time employee cover for me while I went under the vacuum to have the fat in my saddle bags, inner knees and rear deltoid's removed. It was an uneventful procedure, which I drove myself to and from. I laid on the couch the remainder of the day and only used one pain pill. I was back to work the next morning. I never told Matt that I had the procedure and because our relationship had become strictly platonic by then, he never saw or felt the results but they were so obvious to me! Had I known how to eat properly I would have been able to maintain them.

Sadly, I was still a raging anorexic and bulimic, eating and stuffing my feelings with food or taking dangerous laxatives to get the excess calories out of my body. Without understanding the long-term consequences of these choices, I inadvertently damaged my intestines and the appearance of my skin in those areas. It is only in the last few years that I have begun to heal my intestines and have boosted my immune system. The 28 feet of intestines that we all were born with house almost all of our entire immune system. I wound up having two more liposuction treatments after the first one because I really thought it was my only alternative. Boy, was I wrong!

MARCH 2005

The month of March holds quite a number of significant events that helped to frame my life. My oldest brother was born at the end of March 1948 on the 27th. If you believe in the conception calendar's accuracy, which instructs us to add 3 months and one week to our date of birth to determine our conception date, then he would have been conceived on July 4th the year prior! To me, it's a kind of a funny but understandable date since it was a holiday where I am certain booze was flowing. However it's a bit ironic because the birth of a child hardly resonates with one's Independence!

It was over the weekend of March 25th, 2005, that I attended my first White Party in Palm Springs, California; the largest and oldest gay dance party in America.

Stew, my ex-husband, and I were living in Santa Fe, New Mexico and had attended our first circuit party a month earlier when we heard about the White Party in Palm Springs. I was head over heels in love with this "circuit" music and couldn't imagine how amazing I'd feel if I spent an entire weekend dancing at one of these events. I'm sure I didn't have to force Stew to want to go, as he seemed to be enjoying the attention that we both got while we were there. We were both competitive body builders by now and both looked the part.

I happened to mention to a friend of ours, Ted, that we were planning to fly our 6-seater plane (Stew was a pilot and just had to have his own plane!) out to Palm Strings when he told me that he had always wanted to go to that party as well. Stew quickly agreed that Ted should join us and we flew out a few days before to get ready for the three-day party.

Since this was our first time at White Party, we bought weekend passes and planned on attending all the dance and pool parties. I bought every piece of sexy white clothing I could find, worked on my tan, ate my six meals a day, and was as fit as I could possibly be. I, of course, had a stash of new white boots and every piece of costume jewelry that I could find at Claire's accessories! I was ready to party!

My level of excitement was frenetic; I could barely keep my clothes on waiting to walk into a dance party with 3000 hot men! And walk in I did! During that period there were only a handful of women who attended the White Party so we were definitely noticed.

Most of the women were lesbian and perhaps there was a stray straight woman accompanying her gay boyfriend, but trust me when I tell you that Stew and I were the only straight couple there, and for sure the only bodybuilding straight couple! We really stood out, and if I do say so myself, I was the only *true* "dancing queen" there!

We were instantly a hit and actually met people there who are still great friends in my life today. It was a whirlwind and so much fun. We were some of the first people to arrive at the parties and always the last ones to leave. My life changed for good the next night at the official White Party held in the Convention Center.

It was sometime in the early morning, maybe around 2:00am, when I had what I call an *'epiphany'*. I was really high and happy and was dancing to my heart's content, when I heard a voice that said these exact words; **"Move to Palm Springs and train Gay Men!"**

I know it sounds bizarre, but when I heard the words a second time and it appeared that no one else heard what I was hearing, I realized that I was being sent a message. I remember having a body flush of goose bumps and thinking that this was suddenly to be my mission in life!

The next day while Stew and I were enjoying our first White Party T-dance in the lot across from Hunter's Bar, our friend Ted was at Hunter's. He met a guy who he really liked and who liked him back. Later that year Ted would decide to move to Palm Springs and that's where the real fun began.

Meanwhile, back at the T-dance, I was surrounded by men in cut-offs and not much else. I had on a pair of white denim Daisy Dukes, a white lace vest, and a great pair of white high-heeled boots. At some point one of the guys who recognized me from one of the five other dance and pool parties came up and asked me why I was still wearing my vest. I said that I didn't want to offend anyone or get arrested! He said no one will mind and no one cares! New words to my ears!

I love the human body and feel very comfortable naked so the idea appealed to me. He helped me pull the vest over my head, folded it and handed it to my husband, who promptly put in through his belt loop and I continued to dance, sans top! The guys around me were all cheering. I had a great tan and always tanned topless so I had no tan lines. I was probably about 8% body fat making me totally toned. I have always had very highly developed pectoral muscles, which made my chest a showcase, of sorts. I'd have to say that I got a thumbs up and a 10 for a score, if anyone was judging.

As the evening wore on, many men came up to me to tell me that I looked beautiful. A few men had never seen women's breasts before and interestingly asked *my husband* if they could feel my breasts. No one seemed to ask me, but I was so comfortable and relaxed that I gave them a head nod, indicating that it was okay to look and touch! It was one of the coolest moments of my life. It was really a beautiful thing and not at all dirty or kinky or overly sexualized. Not that those things aren't great in the right setting, but this was more of a respect and appreciation thing. I was in 7th Heaven!

After our last closing party of the weekend and with about six hours of sleep, Ted, Stew, and I got back in our plane and flew home. We were up at about 20,000 feet when I told Stew about the "voice-in-my-head-message" I had heard during the White Party. He looked over at me and with one raised eye-brow said, "Honey, you were really high!" to which I responded, "Yes, I was, and I also know what I heard!"

I knew I had to move to Palm Springs and said to him, "Honey, I've got to move there, I'm not sure if you do, but I can't deny the message!" A little more than a fourteen months later we moved to Palm Springs and I started on my life's mission!!

March 2006

Stew and I went on our 2nd Atlantis cruise in March, this time cruising the Caribbean. We had met some amazing folks on the first cruise in 2005 and had arranged to meet some of them on this one. We flew into Ft. Lauderdale, drove to West Palm Beach to see my youngest brother Joel and his family. We spent a few days with them before boarding our ship.

One couple that we had met on the first cruise, Mark and Mike, were sailing with us again. When we met them on the Mediterranean cruise, we had just competed in a body building show and between the two of us had about 10% body fat! Both of these handsome gay men were body builders as well and we quickly became not only fast friends who ate six times a day, but great dance partners too! We spent most of the cruise hanging out together day and night and even went on a few excursions with them unless we stayed up till sunrise and were the last four standing on deck! They referred to themselves as M & M with nuts if you catch my drift. I'm happy to say that they are still friends of mine today, but we are long overdue for another cruise!

March, as they say, goes out like a lamb, so onto April Showers.

APRIL

APRIL 2006

April Showers bring May flowers. In this case it brought Easter. And, in 2006 Stew and I were again back in Palm Springs for our 2nd White Party. Ted, who had now moved to Palm Springs with his new boyfriend, invited us to house sit for them the week before White Party and the week after! It could not have been a more welcome invitation. We were going to experience Palm Springs itself, not just the inside of the convention center and the lot across from Hunters, or the bars on Arenas, but the city itself.

Sadly, I must say that Stew was not impressed. He did not care for mid-century Modern Architecture or the desert landscape. He was a Texan and it seems that California Dreamin' and Texas reality don't mix well. But, I was in Heaven. As a matter of fact, as a Sinatra freak and lover of Mid-Century art and Mid-Century as a lifestyle, I was ecstatic! I also adore Palm Trees and see them as tall guards watching over and protecting us, making me feel safe and secure. I'm not really crazy about the mountain range that borders the city itself, but love those same mountains down valley. It's a shame, but those disparate feelings ended up being a large part of the reason that things didn't work out between Stew and me, but that's for a later time.

So, the week prior to White Party, Stew and I found our way around the city. We had already joined World Gym and because we had been seen out and about town, we were making new friends left and right. The two of us were creatures of habit and we had rituals that we followed religiously. One of them was to have coffee every day at the Starbucks at Ramon and Sunrise after our workout. We usually saw many of the same guys from the gym or the clubs. And trust me, we stood out. People were fascinated with us because they thought that I was Steve's beard or the other rumor; that I was a drag queen/transsexual! Yep, it's true! But I must confess after seeing some of the most gorgeous women that I've ever seen, only to be told that they were a man, I felt like I was being paid the highest of compliments. Go Figure!

Ted had now lived in Palm Springs for almost six months and knew the city well. He told us about this club called Toucan's and we ventured off the first Thursday night to see what all the hype was about. This is the night that I say the "**Dancing Queen of Palm Springs was born!**"

We arrived at Toucans about 10:30p.m. and parked in the lot adjacent to the bar. When I opened the door to the car and heard the music coming from the bar I immediately started to dance in the parking lot, something I had never done before. I danced my way up to the two closed front doors. I pulled open the right door, only to see another set of doors. Now, rather than open one door, I, who grew up in Buffalo, New York, home of the saloon, *pushed* both doors open simultaneously. As I entered I was sending the airflow towards the patrons, who felt the cool air blowing in on them. Because the bar was filled to capacity it caused them all to look towards the entry.

I knew I had an impact because the looks on the patron's faces immediately brightened up. I was still dancing and danced my way right past them doing what is now referred to as the "**Jill Dance!**" I danced my way through the crowd right to the center of the dance floor, where I broke into one of my famous dances. I danced non-stop for at least 20 minutes until Stew brought me my Cosmo, my drink of choice right then.

Believe it or not, I was a Cosmo girl at that time and would have two of them a night whenever I was dancing. Doug, who was the greatest Cosmo maker in the world and one of the best bartenders at Toucans, never disappointed! I'm sorry to say that he has retired and as a result I've switched to only drinking champagne and have never had another Cosmo again! Truthfully, I'll occasionally try one of them even now if I'm at a bar or club that doesn't serve champagne or Proseco but I am always very disappointed. Miss you, Doug!

As a result of that night, Toucan's became the go to hot-spot for Stew and me. We were there every Friday and Saturday night year round unless we were out of town. We would occasionally go on Tuesday night for Two-for-Tuesday's as well. We would typically arrive around 11:00pm after spending about an hour at Sammy G's in downtown Palm Springs, dancing to the Evaro Brothers Band before heading to Toucan's.

I can't tell you how many people thought that Stew and I owned Toucan's, which was hilarious to me. Simultaneously, I think it's amazing how often people would say, "the place isn't the same when you're not here!" I didn't really comprehend the affect that we were having because I was just having so much fun.

During the 2nd White Party weekend there was an after-hours party at a club called Heaven which was located in Sun Plaza on Palm Canyon Drive. Of course we attended the event being the dutiful White Party people that we were and I remember the club being jam-packed.

A few weeks later when we were back in Palm Springs we headed down to Heaven at about 1:45am after dancing at Toucan's. I was still hungry for more dancing but, as it wasn't White Party weekend, the club was pretty empty, save for other dancing queens like me! Stew and I walked in and an energy came over me like nothing I had ever felt before. It was a combination of deja-vu and a spiritual energy, which I found so powerful that I had to succumb to it.

I turned to Stew and said, "I don't know why but I think I am supposed to go on stage and dance!" He said, "Go do what you have to do." So, up I went. I climbed the stage stairs and went right out to the middle of the stage and began to dance, alone.

There were maybe a few dozen gay men on the dance floor and another dozen or so at the bar and of course, Stew. I danced for the next 90 minutes, and perhaps got a few stares but mainly I was simply free to be me. I'm certain that no one imagined that this was the beginning of a new era, at least for me, but it was.

From that day on, for the next seven years, through two new owners and two name changes; from Heaven to Oasis, to Confession, I danced on stage every Friday and Saturday night. Over that time period, thousands of gay men watched me dance and began to recognize me as **The Dancing Queen**, the name they gave me.

Prior to this, I had never danced on a stage, or up on anything elevated in my life. I also have never taken a dance lesson and up until that time had only been a dancer who used my feet to dance but never my hands or upper body. When the new owners took over they built a 2nd bar directly across from the stage and added mirrors to the bar's back wall. And that's when I made a discovery.

With the addition of the mirrors, I was now able to look straight across the room and see myself dancing in the reflection. I noticed that my hands were doing some unusual things and found myself thinking that I was "signing" to the audience. I can't explain this to you because it is based on my spiritual beliefs, but it was as if I truly was sending out a message to each and every gay man in the place. Because this was the only after hours venue in the city every gay man who liked to dance came into the club. It's like everyone knew me. I believe that this is how I became so well known and well received. It's as if I was returning to my tribe after being away for eons.

There is a common reaction in town that applies to strangers as well as friends. If a person meets a new friend the first question they are asked is; "Do you know Jill?" The first response is always; "Everyone knows Jill!"

This next statement might come off as a bit grandiose or bizarre, but if you ask the gay men around town how they feel about me and vice versa, we all say the same things about our feelings for one another. We love one another unconditionally and we feel like we have been connected our entire lives and I don't mean just in this lifetime.

It's the most amazing connection that I have ever felt and it continues on a daily basis. I am so eternally grateful for these feelings and for the love of my community. It makes me want to be a better person for all of you and leaves me hoping that it will lead me to do something very important for all of us. But, back on topic, April will always be one of the most special months in my life as a result of my knowing each and every one of you.

APRIL 2015

My BFF for life, Giselle, a former client, had asked me to drive her to her doctor's appointment in Los Angeles from Palm Springs. I was looking for an excuse to go to L.A. to visit my favorite shoe store, OFF BROADWAY, and quickly said yes. We were planning on heading out early to beat the traffic. We had our plan and looked forward to leaving the next day.

The night before, my sister had called me and out of the blue we ended up talking about the famed fish dishes that she and I had "pretended" to fight over while my mother was alive. It was one of the only things that I coveted and evidently my sister did, too. Strangely the conversation made me melancholy for my mother and her belongings. I mentioned to my sister how sorry I was that I hadn't taken anything that really reminded me of my mother.

That's when my sister really surprised me. She said; "Well you were supposed to get those rings." "What rings", I said. "You know the three rings that belonged to Nonni, Mom, and Dad."

And then I remembered. My mom used to wear my deceased grandmother's 1940's cocktail ring and her own simple gold wedding band. Then, when my Dad died, she decided to wear all three rings on one finger and used a bread tie to hold them together.

"Jeez, that's right, what happened to them?" I said.

"Someone from the Nursing Home must have stolen them. We never found them in her room and they had claimed no knowledge of them." She replied.

I hung up the phone and really felt disappointed and kind of shaken-up.

The next morning Giselle arrived close to 8am. She was on the phone when I answered the door and looked at me to say, "I'll be right off." I nodded to say that I understood, no worries. Giselle was wearing the coolest jean jacket I had ever seen and it fit her perfectly. I was so envious because all my life I have wanted to look cool in a jean jacket but it's never happened. As a matter of fact I had just given away my whole collection of them when I moved nine months ago.

As soon as Giselle got off the phone I told her how great she looked in that jean jacket and she laughed and said; 'Thanks, but it's yours", and then I remembered. When I was moving into my own apartment after Stew's and my divorce, I went through all my clothes and had huge piles to give away. Giselle had always loved clothing from the 70's and loved anything made of blue jean. She found eight jean jackets in my piles of clothing and took all of them home. This was one of them, but I didn't recognize it and I said that I thought she was mistaken and asked to see the label.

When she took off the jacket, I saw that it was a label that my mother always wore. That is why I didn't remember it. At the same moment she said, "Oh, and by the way, I found something you lost!"

Okay, now *I* was really lost!

"What do you mean?" I asked her as she reached out her arm to hand me something. I automatically extended my palm and she gently placed a set of rings into it.

I took one look at them and knew that they were not mine. They were so old fashioned that I assumed (there it is again) that they belonged to her or someone who was older, like her mom. I immediately began to hand them back to her, saying; "I think they must belong to your MO.........and it struck me like a knife, they weren't her mother's, they were *my* mother's and I began to sob!

I had not remembered their existence till last night! Now, a mere 12 hours later, as if she were responding from the grave, they were returned to me, evidently, the rightful owner!

Talk about Freaky! And Amazing! And Lucky!

I was flabbergasted and over-joyed.

Giselle and I both stood there crying, hugging, and laughing.

But that's only part of this great story. Here's how these rings originally came to me:

Two years earlier, when I helped de-construct the place that my parents called home for almost 60 years, I had chosen to take nothing. I had my memories and that was really enough for me. I did not enjoy the majority of my early life and had not been a happy person. I did not need any reminders of that part of my life. I was happy to just help clean the place out and say goodbye forever.

My job was to go through all of her clothes, which was going to be quite a feat for you see my mom and I both collect things. I collect boots and have over 130 pair, so trust me when I tell you that my mom had *collections* of clothing as well and all the accessories that go with them. It was a huge job that took me over four days to sort out. I found only three items that I wanted for myself: a 60's dress, a 70's blazer, and a petite-sized jean jacket. I never ended up wearing the jacket and it ended up in one of the piles of clothing that I was giving away when I was moving into my own place.

Giselle, who had 2 teenage boys, was informed that a student had come to school with bed bugs. The school requested that parents wash every item of clothing, bed-sheets, towels etc., in boiling hot water, not once, but twice. After washing them they were to be dried at high heat for hours and recommended that they use the large machines at a laundromat.

She had done exactly that, jean jacket and all. Now, if the pocket of the jacket not been buttoned down, the rings could have fallen out or been lost to her or found by someone else and never returned to me. Or even crazier, the jean jacket could have gone to Goodwill and they would have been lost to me forever.

But instead, these rings were clearly meant to be with me and for me. All I know is that I will be forever grateful to my dear friend Giselle for being so honest; to my sister for reminding me of what was rightfully mine; and to my mother for speaking from the grave. May you be so fortunate some day!

MAY

MAY 10, 1992
Now, For May Flowers

In 1992 I was living in Albuquerque, New Mexico. I had been seeing Robert, the Borderline Personality guy, and things were getting really hairy. It was obvious that the relationship was coming to an end and actually did so at the end of April.

I had been doing some remodeling in my casita and was now looking for a renter. It was at this time that Jack, who later became my first husband, moved into my casita and essentially into my back yard. It was over coffee one morning in May that Jack confessed that he had heard some of the fights that Robert and I had been having. He told me that he had been tempted on a number of occasions to beat the shit out of Robert for treating me so badly. He didn't know that we had broken up.

Jack referred to Robert as a bully. In thinking back on it, I have come to realize that this was a pattern for me. I have attracted a number of men over the years that were bullies and along the way, came to the realization that my dad was a classic bully as well. I have allowed myself to be abused by them and just like any self-fulfilling prophecy; I waited to be rescued or to become the victim of my own circumstances. Today, I believe that I have finally broken that pattern and am very grateful.

The fact that Jack recognized this quality in Robert I am sure endeared him to me immediately and most likely led me to believe that he was going to be the man who would rescue me, the damsel in distress! It was truly one of the first times in my life that I thought someone besides a teacher was going to stand up for me. Up until this time I had been fighting my own battles and not exactly winning.

At the time, in an attempt to get over Robert, I focused my attention on a waiter who worked at one of the most popular restaurants in town. I would go to dinner there by myself, ask for his table, where we'd flirt with one another on a regular basis.

He had mentioned that he liked Lyle Lovett, and told me that Lyle was going to be playing in Santa Fe at an outdoor venue. He said that he'd been thinking about going. I loved Lyle and when I heard his wish, decided to be proactive and bought two tickets for us to go. A few days before the concert he called to tell me that he had to work and couldn't go. He didn't really sound very sincere or sorry and I remember feeling so hurt and disappointed. I didn't make a lot of money back in those days and it was a bit of a stretch for me to have bought such expensive tickets.

The next day, as I was brooding in my backyard over the waiter, Jack came through the back gate on his way to his casita. We greeted one another and, being the good guy he was, he noticed that I was struggling with something. We began to spontaneously talk. He was such a good listener and so attentive that he immediately put me at ease. We chatted for a good long time and I finally told him why I was so glum. He assumed it was about Robert, but I corrected him and told him about the waiter.

I was touched by Jack's gallant behavior. Thinking back, I realize he was probably the first man who ever made me feel that he was on my side. I guess you can say that he was my hero; he was going to rescue the princess in the tower. All I know is that my heart really softened in that moment and I looked at him in a totally new light. It's so funny how that happens, but it was very real for me and affected many of my decisions in the months to follow. Jack asked which concert I had bought tickets for and I told Lyle Lovett. Lyle certainly had a following back then but was still a fairly obscure person and I doubted that he would know who he was. I just about died when he told me that Lyle Lovett was one of his favorite singers. Now, this might have been a great line, but it felt more like a sign to me. I asked him if he would like to be my guest and I was tickled pink when he said he would! We made arrangements to go that weekend.

It was a warm spring day when we drove the 60 miles from Albuquerque to Santa Fe. On the drive up we started seeing clouds gathering and hoped that the concert, which was outdoors, would not get rained out. We arrived early and sat on the bleachers just chatting away.

We were both very excited to be with one another and there was a lot of energy surrounding us. We were so anxious to hear Lyle in person and excitedly awaited the start of the concert. About half way through the show it started to sprinkle making it the perfect time for the two of us to snuggle under his extra sweatshirt. Our legs had been touching one another prior to this and the sexual energy was intense.

By this time the concert was really rocking and we were both singing along with Lyle. We were having a marvelous time. We could even see Julia Roberts in the wings, smiling and bopping around to the music. And when Lyle dedicated the song Fiona to her, everyone in the audience was beaming. It turns out that Lyle Lovett and Julia Roberts had been secretly dating and the weekend of that concert was to be their first public appearance. Many of us were fascinated with Julia Roberts, so this felt like a personal win! The true irony is that Julia and Lyle both married and divorced one another the same days that Jack and I married in June of 1993 and divorced in March of 1995! I have no idea what any of this means if not just a great coincidence but it sure makes for an interesting twist in my life's story!

A few weeks later, after spending almost every evening together, we finally consummated our relationship. However it would be a month before we realized that the rubber really had broken, and I would find myself pregnant! More about that in July!

MAY 13, 2013

Stew and I had been married for some time and had recently separated. We were still great friends and it was now 2013. We decided we would walk the Camino de Santiago, a pilgrimage that the four characters in the movie, "The Way" had made famous.

After a ten-month trial separation from Stew, I was to meet him at the airport in Madrid. From there, we would fly to Pamplona and then take a taxi to the last town in the northwest of France, Saint Jean Pied de Port. From there we would begin the 500-mile backpacking trip ending in Santiago de Compostela, Spain where the remains of Saint James are buried.
Stew and I agreed to all of this in text messages earlier that January after he had watched the movie; "The Way" which I had recommended to him. What happened in the Madrid airport ironically was a prelude to this adventure.

I flew from Palm Springs across the U.S. to Madrid while Stew flew from Houston to Madrid. Neither one of us had been overseas since 2005 when we had taken our first gay cruise and were quite excited to be on the road again.

We had neglected to get a phone package that allowed us to use our phones so we had to trust that our flights would be on time. My plane was on time but as I was arriving an hour after Stew was to have landed, I hoped he'd be waiting for me at the gate to proceed to Pamplona. I really needed to use the bathroom before I got off the plane but figured I would wait till I got to the Pamplona gate.

Warning, do not wait to use the facilities in European airports because you will end up walking for 20 minutes before you get to the train that will take you to another terminal where you have to walk the full concourse to find your gate and in this case your estranged husband........and finally, a bathroom!

I also forgot to mention that all the bathrooms that I saw during this walk were not open for business. So, when I got to gate 72 and happily saw Stew waiting for me the only thing I could do was to give him a quick hug and kiss and ask where the bathroom was. I did my business, and sadly left my favorite scarf in the bathroom before returning to him to say a true hello. We were really happy to see one another and our tears kind of said it all, but just as we were going to hug, the beautiful sunny day that had greeted me 30 minutes earlier disappeared. It was replaced by dark black clouds and a deluge of rain followed by the largest crack of thunder. This phenomenon occurred just as our arms were going around each other's backs!

This happened in a mere second and we both jumped along with everyone else in the airport! I will never forget saying to him, " The Gods have spoken and I guess this is as good a time as any for a cleansing!"

I really believe that signs are signs and this one was pretty much in our faces. I thought to myself that this was going to be one interesting journey! That was just the tip of the iceberg. What we did not know at the time was that our luggage was sitting out on the tarmac getting soaking wet. We were on the plane when I saw it sitting on the luggage cart. At the same moment, we both realized that neither of our suitcases was waterproofed. What a great way to start a 500-mile trek, right? As good travelers, we both realized that there was nothing that we could do and figured we'd have to use the dryer at the hotel to dry our belongings, right?

Wrong.

The quaint little hotel where we stayed in southern France had limited heat. We asked the owner of our hotel if we could use the dryer to dry our wet belongings and let me tell you our stuff was really wet. He told us that they did not have a dryer and that we would need to hang the clothes in our room, which was ice cold. I was literally shaking and Stew was no warmer, even after taking a tepid shower.

This was mid May and the mean temperatures were usually in the 60's or 70's. Oh, did I forget to mention that when we landed in Pamplona the temperatures had fallen about 30 degrees and it was now 40 degrees outside? By the time we made it to our hotel in Saint Jean, it was dark and cold just like the hotel!

It took two days for our clothes to dry, making us two days late beginning our journey. Things were not really looking or feeling so good.

Did I mention that the rain had turned to snow? Oh, yeah, it's a fact. Believe it or not, this was the first time in over 150 years of recorded temperatures that it had snowed in this region! Being from Buffalo, this did not make me very happy. On day three, the sun came out and our belongings were finally dry enough to start our Camino. We were **our** Way. However, the minute we were out of the sun, it was plenty cold and I was wearing every stitch of clothing that I had brought.

I had moved to Southern California to get away from this kind of weather and it was late spring in Spain. Preparing for my trip I had read the book written by Shirley McLane, called of all things, 'The Camino'. She had made this same trek in the 90's during May and June. In her case there were record-breaking days in the high 90's nearing 100 degrees! I sadly assumed a truth (you know the old saying about assumptions making an ass-u-me!) and imagined that I would be way too hot, but never in a million years believed I'd be way too cold!

The day before we left, we packed up anything that we didn't need and sent it ahead to Santiago, where our trek would end. If you know me or have seen me out and about you quickly learn that I have two sets of footwear, workout shoes and high-heeled boots. The fact that I was going to be in walking/trekking boots for 6 weeks was a really weird concept for me. I had brought along my favorite boots and really struggled with whether or not I should carry them in my backpack or send them ahead. Of course Stew, being so practical and still my husband, raised one eyebrow as he nudged me to send them to Santiago, which I reluctantly did. These, along with everything else were my staple, my high-heeled, boots

My trek would end 256 miles later when I developed a condition known as plantar fasciitis in my left heel. Ironically the best treatment for plantar fasciitis is to wear high heels, which takes the pressure off of the heel! This is one of many examples of me not listening to myself and being a people pleaser.

My left foot (excuse the movie reference) was excruciating. I feel there are no accidents or coincidences in our lives so I began researching the two different sides of our bodies and how they inter-react. One of the modalities that I studied shared an age-old belief that the left side is our female side. Hmmm? This was starting to get interesting. On the other hand, as a right-handed woman, my right side has always been more defined and dominant. My right breast and right thigh are larger than their left counterparts. So, for the first time in my life, I found myself wondering if there was a deeper message to my left-sided plantar fasciitis.

The right side of the body is linked to male attributes. I have always been very close to men and have not had a large number of female friends in my life. Those that I do have I tend to have for life. In a way, I have always felt that I could not relate to women and saw them as weak and silly, and found that I didn't have much in common with them. I believe that this springs from my family of origin and their lack of honoring women and their automatic elevation of tough males in their society.

Here I was on this trip with Stew to see if our 10-month separation made a difference in the way we felt about each other and if there was any hope of the two of us getting back together. Talk about moving forward! I used Google to find out what information I could about foot injuries and the psyche and was not surprised to learn that according to one author it's associated with having difficulty moving forward.

Therefore, "moving forward" could be seen as taking the next step to divorce, which evidently was causing me pain! I'm sure that there are many other ways of interpreting this but this is what resonated best for me. And due to the fact that it was me who wanted the initial separation, then it very well could be up to me to ask for a divorce especially since Stew had made it very clear that he did not want one.

Stew, who had not been feeling any spiritual connection to this pilgrimage we were on, suggested one non-snowy afternoon that we might pack it up and go home! I was truly flabbergasted by this because neither one of us were quitters and as much as this heel pain hurt, I figured I would just tough it out, like I had done so many other times in my life.

In the back of my mind, I had also been questioning my decision to keep walking based on two things. One; I am a personal trainer who is on my feet 6-8 hours a day and Two; As The Dancing Queen I love to dance and wondered if I was causing any long term damage that would affect my ability to work my **body** and my **spirit** through dancing!

These were critical activities that I would not want to give up so when he suggested that we go home, I agreed! We told the small group of our new life-long friends about our plans to abandon and found them to be in utter disbelief.

We had a goodbye dinner and Stew and I boarded the next bus we found that would take us to the nearest city with a train station. Since we had sent our all of our belongings to Santiago, we now had to go retrieve them. We already had plane reservations from Santiago back to Madrid.

We took the bus to Leon, a beautiful city where I was on a mission to find a pair of high-heeled boots to cure my plantar fasciitis. I knew that I always felt better in high heels and had been a back-packer in sneakers long enough.

I went to every single shoe store in Leon and finally found an adequate pair. And much to my surprise was immediately pain free minutes after putting them on. Sitting here now makes me wonder why I didn't just tell Stew that I wanted to continue the walk since my foot no longer hurt, but, that clearly wasn't in the cards.

This is where the story takes a turn.

After we had checked into our hotel, Stew was anxious to contact the travel agent who had made our original reservations. She had no trouble changing my ticket but wasn't able to do so for Stew. He was not happy about this at all and it showed.

Originally, I had wanted to go to both Spain for the Camino and to England to visit my English gay roommate. He had been living with me in the condo that Stew and I had when we separated. I had mentioned this to Stew but couldn't quite figure out how to do both trips trip together due to time constraints and costs and I settled on Spain and "The Way."

But, now with the change of plans, I was going to fly to England and spend 15 days with my friend, while Stew was going to fly back to his home in Texas. At the end of my 15 days I would fly back to Madrid where I would finally fly home.

The agent continued to try to book Stew's return trip to no avail. She finally told him that he would have to find a local travel agency to book his ticket and that it was too late so he would have to wait until the next day. I don't know why but this made Stew very angry and it showed in his stride the next morning when we were on our way there.

I was wearing my new boots that morning as we headed to the travel agency. Stew was walking really quickly and although I was pain-free for the first time in three weeks still asked him numerous times to slow down. Finally we were walking side by side and a few minutes later I realized that he wasn't next to me on this rather narrow sidewalk. I turned around to see what he was doing.

I took one look at his face and knew what was about to happen. I said to him, "You're not leaving The Camino, are you?" and I will never forget the look in his eyes or the feeling in my stomach when he gently and quietly said, "No."

We both stopped dead in our tracks and stood there blocking the sidewalk. I could tell he was a little embarrassed and uncomfortable and I was feeling very uncertain and disappointed to realize that I was now the quitter and he was going to be the hero!

That probably sounds awful and it makes me a little embarrassed for myself that I thought this way but I am nothing if not truthful. We went and got coffee to process this but it really was a turning point that I did not recover from until I left a few days later when I flew to England.

I say recover, but I really did not enjoy myself in England and kind of fell apart while I was there. Stew in the meantime managed to become a hero of sorts, gathering new female friends along the way and writing about it in the blog that we had both started prior to leaving the States.

Looking back, I guess I could have stayed and attempted to finish but it was not to be and is something that I don't honestly regret because I think the whole purpose of my having watched the movie "The Way", was to get Stew to walk The Camino for himself.
I just hate being a quitter and in a way, quitting the Camino has allowed me to be a bit looser and sloppier with my commitments. This is something that I am having to work on for the first time in my life and I don't like it!

MAY 25, 2007

Ah, the month of May for me has some very powerful days, the most significant being May 25th. In 1947 my parents got married on May 25th at City Hall in downtown Buffalo, New York. Many years later their firstborn, my brother Jerry, and his wife Lucy got married the same day. But as life has it, May 25, 2007 also changed my life as it marks the first night that I spent in California as a new resident.

Stew and I had continued to travel back and forth from Santa Fe to Palm Springs ever since our first visit. We had bought a lot and were building a house in the Mesa District. Until it was complete, we got our own small apartment where we stayed with our friend Ted, who had moved into his new boyfriend's house. They had graciously given us full use of the casita in their back yard.

It became our home away from home. We would spend almost every other weekend there for close to a year before deciding to move to Palm Springs in

May of 2007. The weeks before our move, Stew was in Palm Springs doing business and making plans for the new home that we were building there while I was back home in Santa Fe packing up our life, preparing for our move.

Stew returned on May 19 to find most of the house packed up. We held a huge garage sale that weekend, ridding ourselves of the excess we had acquired over the years and made quite a bit of money to boot! I had it in my mind that we would leave on Thursday the 24th and drive into Palm Springs mid day on the 25th, unpack our car and truck, take a nap and be at Toucan's that night. Stew told me I was crazy, but I had faith. And sure enough we were in the car on the 24th and on our way.

Interestingly, we had car problems just as we were about to enter California. Looking back on it now, I think that the two hours we waited for AAA was most likely Stew's resistance to moving to California. It was a miserably hot day and we had a long wait, putting a lot of stress on us both. We did not enter California as happy campers!

But, as things go, we managed to get into town, unpack and *were* at Toucans that night by 10:00pm I remember how excited I was. I was running around telling everyone that "tonight will be my first night as a California resident!" Of course most of them thought I was nuts. In their mind they saw me every other weekend, so how could May 25th be the first night as a Californian? I had to tell them that we had been visiting all those weekends and actually lived in New Mexico. It was actually pretty funny to see the looks on their faces when they got it.

JUNE

June is my birth month so you might imagine that it has many twists and turns to it, and you are right! As Julie Andrews says in my favorite movie, "The Sound of Music", "Lets start at the very beginning."

I was born on June 21, 1955 at 12:30pm. I share this birthday with some notable people, like Juliette Lewis, Jean-Paul Sartre, Benazir Bhutto, Jane Russell, and Edward Snowden. Prince William was also born on this day and now that we know so much more about Diana, I feel very connected to him. Diana was also an anorexic/bulimic who had a strong affiliation to the gay community. I have always felt close to her even before I knew any of her secrets. Her story, her pain, her insecurity and inadequacies are all fascinating. She was strong yet weak, beautiful, yet hated her looks and was a light-worker who had a dark side.

According to many astrological sources, being born on June 21 makes me a Gemini whose sign are the twins. But, depending on which source you believe I can also be considered a Cancer since I was born on the cusp, or in-between 2 signs. If that is the case, I guess it makes me a double twin! Can it get anymore confusing?

Yes, it can! Most sources report that June 21st is the first day of summer and the Summer Solstice or the longest day of light. This always made me feel special and very happy. But according to other sources as of 2020, the first day of summer will now be June 22nd, making me feel bummed out and disappointed. How can that be? How can you just change the day on me? I mean the first day of summer is the longest day of light or the shortest night. I have always loved that especially since so many of you say that I am a light source and a light being. Does this mean that I only have 3 more years to be this person? I sure hope not!

While there is all this light energy coming through on June 21st, back in 1955, on that day, there was another special energy coming through as well called Mercury Retrograde (MR). It has taken me along time to understand what it means to be born under the energy of Mercury Retrograde but a simple way to understand it is to say that we interpret information differently and tend to think and communicate in a unique way as well.

Three to four times a year, Mercury goes into Retrograde which allows us to look back over the last 3 months to see if we have been accomplishing our goals. If so, we move forward or if not, we kind of go backwards in time to have a re-do, if you will. Unfortunately, most people don't know about this opportunity and can stay stuck in the past, making the same choices and ultimately the same mistakes over and over again.

It is believed that communication, learning and travel are all affected negatively or positively during these times. It is interesting that three presidents chose to believe the energies surrounding M.R. and did not sign any contracts or legally binding papers in a retrograde period. These presidents were John F. Kennedy, Ronald Reagan and William Jefferson Clinton!

I only learned about MR ten years ago and ever since have begun to comprehend why my life has gone the way it has. I was able to look back at the MR calendar and compare those dates with significant events in my life. It was both shocking and eye opening to realize how many of these events took place during a retrograde period. It was then that I came to believe that there really are no accidents! At least that's the way that I choose to look at my life.

When I was born, my mother had symptoms that troubled her doctors. They deduced that she had Mononucleosis and told her that she was contagious and was told not to hold me. Can you imagine telling this to a new mother? It's rather overwhelming and harsh for both parties. And if the mother has unresolved issues, this mandate can lead to a lot of guilt, which I believe was the situation in my case.

There are volumes of books that have been written about the psychological issues that develop from the lack of motherly touch and I am here to say that I agree with their findings. I have always had a great need to touch people and to stimulate myself as well. I am know as a hugger and typically hug every person I meet. In fact I feel odd if I don't. I also use a light touch to make a connection in a crowd of people that I know. I try to be as non-invasive as possible and feel I can recognize when this touch would be considered inappropriate or rude and don't ever rock that boat. I knew that I had the need to touch but it was only about ten years ago that my mother told me about this so-called Mononucleosis condition! It helped me understand myself better.

As a result of my mother following her doctors orders not to hold me, she had no other choice but to bottle feed me and propped the bottle in my crib when it was time for me to eat. It would be almost 30 years later that the medical community discovered that bottle propping leads to otitis media, or middle ear infections, which I suffered from most of my life. Psychologists have also come to understand that a child who is not held or nurtured will develop a syndrome know as "failure to thrive" or F.T.T. These children are typically underweight, are poor feeders, have difficulty swallowing and/or are being abused or neglected. I had a hard time gaining weight and had a hard time swallowing most likely due to otitis media. As a matter of fact, I had to have my tonsils removed when I was just three years old, because the doctors thought my swollen tonsils were preventing me from eating.

They believed that my inability to gain weight was a result of chronic tonsillitis but I believe it was from not being held. It was in these early years that I also began to masturbate. It's a well-known fact that all children and babies touch themselves to learn about their bodies. But, I knew from a very early age that masturbation for me was something entirely different. I will go into great detail about this in another month's chapter so I will move on from it at this time.

As an aside, I don't think that my Mother actually had Mono but instead was suffering from Post Partum depression. I say this because of information that I have collected over the years from other relatives and friends. Only recently did I learn that my mother had a miscarriage between my sister and me, which is perhaps why there is a 5½ year gap between us. Was my mother depressed all that time? Were my parents having marital problems? Was my birth a planned pregnancy? Did they want to have more children or was I the first of two accidents? I mean my youngest brother is 5½ years younger than me as well. There was a time in my life that I was very, very angry with my parents and used to kind of harass them. They both looked very uncomfortable and angry when I would ask if I was an accident and of course they never answered the question or accusation as it were! It also could have been the empty nest syndrome: a syndrome where parents get pregnant to avoid intimacy with their spouse/partner but at this point in time I will never know, as both of my parents are deceased.

I also had many breathing issues as a very young child. I believe they stemmed from undiagnosed lactose allergies and middle ear infections, which clogged my sinuses day in and day out. Sleeping was a nightmare for me. I would fall asleep while lying on my left side and shortly thereafter, my left nostril would become completely clogged up causing me to not be able to take in any air on that side which would in turn wake me up. In order to breathe, I learned to roll over onto my right side. After 15 or 20 minutes, the left nostril would clear up and I could go back to sleep. But, sometime later that same night the same thing would happen all over again and I would flip and flop all night long in order to breathe.

I'm certain I never got a full night's sleep until I learned a new trick. If I elevated my head by using 2 or more pillows, I could sleep all night long. Little did I know that rather than solving the problem (a Lactose allergy), I instead was creating two new problems; indigestion leading to IBS, and the second; skeletal issues in my neck and lower back. By swallowing nasal mucus my intestines had trouble absorbing nutrients, which caused severe inflammation in my body and was the beginning of both chronic diarrhea and constipation. Using two or three pillows to elevate my head caused me to lose the two naturally occurring S-curves in my spine. This resulted in poor posture and some hip dysplasia. More on that later.

In order to breath properly, I lived in what was called a "croup tent" beginning my long love affair with Vicks Vapor Rub! To this day, I always feel better when I smell Vicks. But, sadly, I think this was also the beginning of my need for attention through illness. I say that because I was an accident-prone child and was in and out of the emergency room starting at age seven when I fell off of a teeter tauter and cracked my head open. Another time I fell off my bike while turning into our driveway and landed on top of a pointed stone that conveniently stuck into the center of my knee. To this day I sill have a scar on my left knee. There are many more times that I was in the E.R., many of which had to do with picking scabs.

I was a champion scab "picker" and wouldn't stop until I made myself bleed. And boy do I mean I was a 'picker'. Around age 3 I was attacked by a ton of large and juicy mosquitos that loved the humidity of Buffalo, New York. For some reason my knees got the best of the bites, especially my left knee. I scratched the bites until they bled and then would wait for the scabs to form before pulling them off again.

I also must confess that I ate my scabs! Yep, it's true, I was that girl! I picked them till they became infected, which they did a lot. One infection was so bad that I had to go back to the E.R. to have the doctor remove part of the cartilage in my left knee. The amazing thing is that when I got chicken pox I did not pick the scabs and therefore do not have any chicken pox scars, which many other people do! That is a small miracle in my world and one that I am grateful for. Without knowing it this too was the beginning of a life long habit of harming the left or female side of my body.

There is now a diagnosis for this condition called Excoriation Disorder. It's classified as a Body-Focused Repetitive Behavior or BFRB. I looked up the definition of the word excoriation and found this meaning; "The act of stripping possessions wrongfully or by force." The corresponding mental symptoms of this syndrome include negative emotions like depression, anxiety, shame and helplessness. It amazed me to read about this diagnosis now because during childhood I was shamed and yelled at by my parents for having these symptoms. This will become more meaningful in understanding where all my energy comes from.

I was also a compulsive hair puller and nail biter all of which are part of this same disorder. I bit my nails daily if not hourly, ripping my cuticles with my teeth until they bled and often times got infected as well. Twice I had to go to E.R. to have a cuticle lanced to remove the infection, but after the second time, I learned to soak the finger in close to boiling hot water where I simultaneously "milked" the infection out of the finger and then covered it in antibiotic cream and a Band-Aid.

As for the hair pulling, I succeeded in pulling out a 2" section on the very top of my head creating a bald spot. This happened in second grade and when the hair began to grow it grew in straight up and made me look like I had a carrot stem growing out of my skull! Not a very good look at any age, let alone at seven! I have a widow's peak as well. Add to that, I had two baby teeth that grew out of my upper gums that looked like fangs when I smiled earning me the nickname, "Eddie Munster". As if all that was not enough, my skin was so translucent that my blood vessels were prominently visible. This earned me a second nickname; Swiss Cheese.

I also have a burn on my left inner calf (there's that left side again) and I subsequently ended up having two plastic surgeries that involved skin grafts. Both of the grafts came from my right buttock cheek. To this day I have a scar on that cheek that is about 4 x 7 inches. I was put in a full leg cast after the first surgery, which I wore for about two months.

As the grafts healed the casts became smaller until I only wore an ace bandage. I could remove it at will and did anytime I wanted to, or needed to pick. I was fascinated with burn treatment care and would watch every move the doctor made as he was debriding the scabs on the skin graft. He was an artist whose moves were all critical as to not form a scar. I studied his moves and replicated them. I learned when to stop pulling the scab so that I did not create scar tissue or damage. It became a game to me and I became as skilled as my doctor.

I must have been a dirty little girl because also got Impetigo, a contagious bacterial skin infection forming pustules and yellow crusty sores. Its name is from the Latin impetere meaning "attack!" Again, another interesting word that goes along with the definition of excoriation. In other words, I was attacking myself.

I was self-destructive. Impetigo was a staph infection of the worse kind back in the day with today's equivalent being M.R.S.A.! I had to keep myself in a quarantine-type state, use special utensils, towels and bed clothing. I think I may have gotten this twice in my childhood and again am amazed that I do not have any scars from this illness. It makes me sad to know that no one in my household wanted to know "why" I was doing what I was doing and that my parents chose to live in denial about my symptoms.

Its also amazing that I did not develop impetigo on the burn on my leg but instead have a very smooth looking permanent scar. For that I am grateful. At that time in my life, when asked what I wanted to be when I grew up, I would respond; "a surgeon." I know this was a result of my experience and I am grateful for it as well. I say this because just a few years later with the onset of puberty I developed acne on my back and being a "picker" could be very scarred today, but I am not! There really are no accidents.

Now onto the significant events that occurred in my birth month...

JUNE 1961

Going back in time, perhaps the most unique thing that happened in June was the train trip that I took with my mother and my sibs back in 1961. In 1959 my grandmother, aunt and cousin moved from Buffalo, NY. to Whittier, CA. the home of President Richard Nixon.

Since my Mom missed her Mother, my parents decided that she would take us kids to visit them once school got out, so off we went. We boarded the train in Buffalo and traveled west stopping in Chicago, IL., where I saw the world's tallest man, John F. Carroll who stood 8ft 5in which was gigantic to little old me who was probably 3ft 3in at best!

From there we changed trains and headed southwest to Santa Fe, N.M. where I saw an American Indian. I will never forget my mother telling me that it was against the law to take a picture of an Indian. She said that the Indians believed that if their picture was taken it would capture their spirit and it would be gone forever. As a result I was instantly afraid of the Indians. They looked powerful and mean and did not smile at me. It made me feel like I had done something wrong which sadly was how I felt most of the time growing up.

While we were waiting for the train to load up the people who were boarding in Santa Fe, a very tall, very somber, Indian man was walking down the platform. I had my nose pressed up against the window and because of his height and my short stature we appeared eye to eye. I will never forget the feeling that entered my body when he looked right at me. It felt like he looked right through me. I shivered then and can remember that feeling now. It was eerie, powerful and exciting all at the same time.

Two days later, we finally made our way to Los Angeles, CA., where my aunt and cousin were waiting for us. Little did I know that I would move to Chicago and Santa Fe in my lifetime, re-creating a pattern that was evidently established in my sixth year of life. The only city that I did not visit on that trip was Atlanta, so I guess you could say I was off course for the three years that I lived there.

As a six year old I remember going to Knott's Berry Farm and of course Disney Land! It was so exciting to be at these humongous theme parks and remember riding the Matterhorn and getting soaking wet at the end when our car made it down to the bottom of the mountain. Thankfully it was a warm day and I didn't get too cold. I also remember going to Pioneer Town where I saw large wooden statues of both Cowboys and Indians.

What I did not remember was driving out to Palm Springs. It would be 47 years later when my aunt would remind me about that trip. She shocked me when she told me that I had not only been to Palm Springs but had also taken a ride up the mountain on the Tram.

She told me that while standing on top of the San Jacinto Mountains, overlooking the entire Coachella

Valley I told my mother; "Mom, I'm moving to California someday!" It was as if I had known even then that Palm Springs held a special energy for me and that I would be returning to my home, to my people; my tribe.

I have often wondered if I had been an American Indian in a past life, let alone one in the Coachella Valley. When I was 18 my B.F.F. and I took a trip to Lily Dale, a psychic community located in southwestern N.Y. State. We made appointments to see a few of the psychics who lived there. Lily Dale is the birthplace of the organized spiritual movement in the United States and is just a mere hour south of Buffalo. The entire community is registered psychics and must live their full time. There's a very quiet and eerie feeling to the place.

While waiting for our appointments, we were encouraged to go down to the gazebo on the lake. A man walked onto the gazebo while we waited and asked if we would like to know about our "spirit guides." To tell you the truth, I had no idea what he was talking about but of course said yes. He told me that I had an Indian as my spirit guide. He said that my guide stood behind me guiding me in all things. He described him as being very tall and that he had one feather in his hair. He told me that I was very lucky to have this guide and in comparison to what he told my friend, who had a less noble guide, I did feel honored.

Flash forward to 2007 when a photographer friend of mine took a series of photos of me. In one of them I look like an Indian Chief. I have a very pronounced widows peak and in this photo, with the faux-hawk I was sporting at the time, the widow's peak looks like a huge feather sticking out of my hair. The lighting on the photo makes my skin look older and rough and I am not smiling which makes my face look very intense. In a way, I think I look a lot like the Indian man who passed by me on the platform and that maybe the eerie feeling that I had was a memory of a past life, and not fear. Just saying..........

JUNE 12, 1993, a spiritual lesson!

On June 12, 1993 I married for the first time to Jack, whom I wrote about in many of the previous months. I thought it would be cool to get married in June. I was born on the 21st, and liked those numbers, but didn't want to get married on my birthday. I checked the calendar to see what day June 12th fell on and I was delighted to see that it fell on a Saturday, giving us our date!

What I didn't tell you is what happened right before I was to walk down the aisle, err garden path. One of Jack's best friends had a lovely home in Albuquerque complete with a beautiful garden. Jack and I did not have a lot of money to spend on a wedding or a reception. Since my parents were throwing us a reception in New York, we decided to have an inexpensive, down-home wedding in her back yard.

We made all the food, rented china, silverware and stemware to at least give it a little charm and invited our closest friends to attend. Our music was based on our first date at the Lyle Lovett concert and I was to walk down the garden path alone once I heard Lyle's voice singing one of our favorite songs. The guests would be standing in the garden awaiting my arrival.

So, there I was in my lovely white palazzo pants and white brocade jacket waiting to walk down the path to my fiancé and soon to be husband. I wanted to be extra classy that day and decided that a white parasol was the way to go. What I didn't know is that it is considered bad luck to open an umbrella or parasol indoors.

I opened the parasol and had it resting on my right shoulder when I heard my cue. I took a deep breath and began to walk thru the door. Now you must be ready to picture this in your mind because what happened was absolutely hilarious.

I walked one or two steps out the door when I was suddenly thrust backwards into the room. Picture the cartoon where there's a bad act on stage and a large hook comes out and drags them offstage! I say this because that is what went through my mind as I went flying backwards into the room!

I was now back in the room, flabbergasted, laughing, crying and wishing that someone else was there to appreciate how hilarious it was, but I was alone. Later when I was telling the story, Jack said that he was worried that I had changed my mind because I had missed my cue even though I had gotten it right when we had practiced the day before. I believe that it was my "universe" and guardians who were basically saying something like, "Don't go out there, you're making a mistake!" especially since it would be a mere 21 months later that Jack and I would get divorced.

JUNE 10, 2000, a body lesson!

On June 10, 2000, I competed in my first body building show in Albuquerque, N.M. I had only attended one bodybuilding show prior to this when I went to watch my first trainer's husband compete. I have to say that I was rather bored and although I had been happy to support her, I left right after his performance. It wasn't all that much different for my first show but the circumstances were certainly more interesting.

Stew and I had prepared for exactly 6 months for my first show. I had worked out, eaten all my meals, taken steroids, diuretics, had practiced my posing routines and had done more cardio than ever before. I was excited, nervous, and exhausted.

Stew had promised that as soon as the show was over he would take me out to eat whatever I wanted. I have to admit that this was foremost thing on my mind. I was an anorexic-bulimic and had focused on food most of my life. I also had no idea how I would do in the show, because I did not have a clue as to what the competition was like. And with all of my body dysmorphia I had no idea that mine could or would be the winning body!

I had entered three categories; Novice Category for people entering their first competition; Master's Category for women over 35 (I was one week away from turning 45) and Open Category for all ages. In my mind I thought that I might be able to win the Master's Category because of my age, but funnily enough came in 3rd for that category!

You are assigned a number in competitions and it just so happened that I was given Number 1. Women's Master's went on stage first and when they called out the winners, I was awarded 3rd place! I felt relieved thinking that the competition was over and I could go eat. I accepted my trophy and went to find Stew to tell him that I was ready to go. With that raised eyebrow he said, " Absolutely not! You have to stay. You are going to win at least two other trophies!"

"What?" I stammered, "Are you serious?"

I had no idea what he meant because I did not realize that I had done so well. He said that I had won the Novice Category and that I most likely would win the Lightweight Open as well! He said I would have to go back on stage to compete with the Middleweight and the Heavy weight winners so that they judges could decide the Overall Winner!

The Overall Winner! You can't be serious. I was truly in shock. I went on to win exactly the awards that Stew had predicted so I truly was Number 1.

I had no way of knowing that I had done so well. I was fixated on going out to eat dessert, the thing I had given up for the last six months. It was hard for me to keep focused and honestly I think I really was in shock.

I had never been awarded any trophy for my body and the attention that I was getting for it was totally overwhelming. Men and women were coming up to congratulate me. Even funnier were the men who were coming up to ask Stew if they could touch my washboard abs! They never asked me, but instead him.

The local news station was back stage and when they found out that Stew was in his late-fifties and I was in my mid-forties they asked if they could interview us for the news. Of course we said yes and they featured our story later that night. So not only was I the over all winner of the show but I was also on TV for the first time in my life!

What I didn't know at the time is that Flex Magazine's photographer had also been in the audience and had taken pictures of all the winners. It would be in the February 2001 issue that my photo would be on page 272! It was truly one of the best nights of my life! Oh, and by the way, at 12:45am June 11, I was finally sitting in Denny's restaurant on Central Ave in downtown Albuquerque where I ate not only one piece of Peanut Butter Pie with extra whipped cream but also a slice of chocolate pie with extra whipped cream and shared a plate of French fries with Stew!

That night I slept like a baby. The next morning we got up and went out to breakfast for my favorite meal of pancakes with real butter and real maple syrup. Then we stopped at a friend's house to do a photo shoot in his backyard where he had my favorite doughnuts. Now there is a funny phenomenon that happens after one competes and it has to do with chemical responses of the body after dieting down for 12 weeks prior to the competition.

The last week before the show you make very specific alterations to your diet. You eat the same types of foods and number of meals the first 3 days, but by Wednesday you begin to take out all salt and begin to drink a lot of water. Depending on the person you may even begin to reduce the amount of carbohydrates that you take in. On Friday if all has gone well, you reduce the amount of water down to about 50oz for the day. Prior to this you might have been drinking 132oz a day.

Since this was my first competition, I also took a mild diuretic, which flushes out even more water from my body. The morning of the show there is a weigh in and at that time it is determined which category you will compete in. The morning of June 10th, I weighed in at 107 pounds, putting me in the lightweight category. Once the weigh in is over, you eat a regular meal which includes salt and water. At this point the body absorbs the salt and water and forces it into the muscles making them firmer and harder. They appear very full and rounded which makes you look great on stage.

After eating the high sugar foods right after the competition, it made my veins pop out and my muscles look fuller and harder than they had been the day before. This made it a perfect time to be photographed. Sadly, I did not know much about posing so the photos from shoot are not very good however the most fascinating thing for me was weighing myself that Sunday night when we got back to Santa Fe.

We had ended the day with my favorite meal of pizza. I don't know what I thought I would weigh but was absolutely floored when I got on the scale and it read 121 pounds! I had gained 14 pounds in 36 hours! I was devastated, but Stew told me not to worry about it explaining that it was water retention from all the sugar and salt that I had eaten. He told me to relax and promised I would be back to my regular weight in a few days.

This was a very hard thing for me to deal with due to my anorexic personality, low self-esteem and my body dysmorphia. As it turns out, it would take *me* almost 3 months before the weight came off and Stew had to eat his words and admit that I did have a very unusual body!

June also is full of other interesting anniversaries and birthdays. Matt was born in June, as was Stew, as well as his father and sister. And our dog Max was put down in June, but more about him in the September's chapter.

JULY

JULY 4, 1990

I moved to Albuquerque, NM. in 1988 where I bought my first house. I was working as the Director of the Inpatient Chemical Dependence Ward for the Charter Hospital Systems and was single, again. There, I met a man named James. He was the head chef for the hospital and was one of three Italian men that I have dated. I am struck by how many men I have dated whose name starts with the letter "J" one more pattern that I have discovered from writing these memoires.

James and I had quite a long, flirtatious, courtship that included Klondike Bars. Let me explain. I would go to the cafeteria every day for lunch and order up some type of healthy meal and on occasion, would treat myself to a Klondike bar. I don't know why this was my favorite type of ice cream but it was. This was 1990 and Dove Bars along with Haagen-Dazs and Ben and Jerry's were the way to go, so how I ended up eating Klondike Bars is beyond me but it definitely caught the eye of James and his employees.

When I would show up in the cafeteria, one of James's workers would evidently go to his office to let him know that I was there. I'd be in line choosing my food when he would suddenly appear. As I would be approaching the cashier, he'd flirtatiously hand me a Klondike bar over the counter. We would both smile and giggle like teenagers in love. This went on for months until he finally got a little more forward and began coming up to my office where I would find a bar sitting on my desk. Now the interesting thing is that these bars never melted! I'm not sure how that worked but I promise you that I never had a sticky, melted mess on my desk! It was all very cute and great fun. I was totally into it and enjoyed the attention and flirtation.

Sometime in early June of 1988, James seemed to disappear and was nowhere to be found. After asking around I learned that he had gone to an inpatient treatment facility for cocaine addiction. I have to say that I was a bit shocked but since I was so smitten with him, I suppose I chose not to see his addictive behavior, let alone my own.

In early July, he was back to work and looked amazing. He was a handsome man to begin with and now with 30 days clean and sober under his belt, looked even better. He asked me out and I of course said yes. Let's put it this way, my boundaries were clearly blurry. Here I was dating another employee, which I am sure was frowned upon by the organization that we both worked for, and I was dating a man who had been out of treatment for less than a week. The red flags were flying and I was a blind as a bat to any of them.

Now that he was clean and sober he seemed more grounded and secure than he had before. Our flirtation grew even stronger and he finally asked me out. Our first date was on July 4, 1990. We were going to dinner at one of nicest restaurants in the city. We were both giddy and happy and I just knew it was going to be the beginning of a good relationship.

We were nervously sitting down at the table when the waiter approached us for our drink order. James quickly chimed in to say, "Have whatever you'd like, it's not a problem for me." This jogged my memory that he had just gotten out of treatment and obviously was not using any substances, including alcohol. I was about to order my standard drink at the time, a glass of red wine, when I heard myself saying, "That's ok, I'll just have water."

I remember thinking to myself that maybe this was a good time for me to quit all the vices I had. I was a smoker, used pot when I could find it, and of course drank alcohol. I did not think that I had an issue with any one of them but it seemed like a good time to just quit cold turkey. I'm sure I imagined that the two of us would be together for a long time and it would be easier if we both remained drug and alcohol free.

James and I had close to a dozen good dates before things went downhill. He was unable to stay drug and alcohol free whereas my own sobriety would last 10 years. It would be years later that I would realize that I had gained my independence on this Fourth of July the way my mother had lost hers on the same date! By mid-July, we had broken up and it was during that time that I decided to attend my first AA meeting. I didn't like the feel of AA and I heard about another group called CODA, or Co-Dependency Anonymous. I started attending those meetings and soon realized that I was a true co-dependent. It was incredibly scary to hear *my* story coming out of the mouths of others. I had no idea that this was *me* but, really, if the shoe fits, wear it. Maybe this is why I now wear boots all the time instead of shoes!

I attended these meetings regularly. Through CODA meetings I heard about another meeting called SAA, Sex Addicts Anonymous. I had often wondered what my issue with sex was as well as the partners I had chosen, but never allowed myself to take those thoughts any deeper. I had been a chronic masturbator since I was a very small child and had not really talked to anyone about it because this was the 80's and people were not upfront about their issues. It was in these meetings that I heard people admit to these same types of behaviors.

I was intrigued and fascinated as well as relieved. Maybe I really wasn't the freak that I thought I was all along. I had had sex with close to 100 people up to this point in comparison to my girlfriends who only admitted to a few encounters. I felt like a slut or, at the very least, a sex addict and thought I was a really sick person. It may be hard for you to believe, but girls have always talked to their B.F.F.'s about their sexual relationships in great detail. I never lied about my adventures and I'm sure I entertained a lot of my friends with my sexual encounters. But sex is sex and the topic of masturbation was totally taboo.

There were no sex toy parties, no sex shops that women frequented, or if there were, they were only for "those girls". Although Playgirl Magazine had been out since 1973, I never knew any women who had bought them, so being at a public meeting where people were sharing their stories about sex and masturbation was very relieving.

I had been a promiscuous young girl, (judging myself) and remember feeling sexually excited with a cousin when I was seven years old. It was on a family visit to my mother's hometown of Binghamton, New York when my older boy cousin invited me to go to the barn on their property. We climbed into the loft and began tickling each other. I was wearing a pair of denim shorts and a white crop top whose little straps fell off my shoulders. It didn't take long for the rest of the top to fall away as well. He pulled me on top of him and we were humping; his hands fondling the tiny breast buds that I had. I remember feeling excited and since I had been masturbating regularly over the last six years could feel the wetness in my vagina.

We were so wrapped up in this moment that neither one of us heard my mother come into the barn until she said the famous words, "Young lady, what are you doing? Come down here immediately!"

I will never forget the shame I felt climbing down that ladder nor the look on her face, which was red, angry, and disgusted. I actually had hay in my hair and my clothes were totally disheveled. She did not talk to me or look at me for hours but I would stay fixated on the sexual feelings that I had, longing for the time that I could feel them again.

It would be sometime later that fall that I began to masturbate with a girl in my neighborhood. She was my best friend and she was the one whose father had sexually abused her until her mother finally divorced him.

She and I were highly sexually aroused. I don't remember whose idea it was to go into the bushes and pull down our pants and start masturbating, but we did and it went on for many months over the summer between second and third grade......until we got caught.

The way it happened is so interesting but understandable if you know how children think. For many months the two of us would climb under a bush that was on the far end of her mother's property. We could see and hear anyone who was approaching and could pull our panties up in time to not get caught.

Perhaps we were too sure of ourselves when we decided that we could masturbate out in the open. Her house was on one side of my uncle's house and my parent's, on the other. We decided to masturbate between my uncle's house and my parent's house. Although we could see and hear anyone who was approaching us, we didn't know that her mother could look out her bedroom window and see us. And that's exactly what happened!

Not knowing that we had been seen made it worse when I was later confronted by my mom. I was in my bedroom doing extra credit reports and was actually drawing and coloring pictures of ships when I heard my mother's footsteps coming up the stairs, making her way to the 2nd floor.

The door to my bedroom was closed when I heard a quick tap and felt the air from the door pushing inwards towards me. Now you must understand that up until that moment everything in my world was going great. I loved doing extra credit assignments and loved drawing pictures of ships. So, I was not expecting what happened next.

"Young lady!" my mother sternly said, "I just got off the phone with Mrs. B. who told me what you and Lee were doing on the side of the house! What do you have to say for yourself?"

At first I thought I was in the middle of a bad dream. I had no idea what she was saying let alone referring to. First off, this had happened hours ago and was already out of my mind. Secondly, I was so baffled by this intrusion and attack that I couldn't focus on what she was talking about. I'm sure I looked perplexed and guilty when I said, "I don't know what you mean?!"

My mother had one of those faces that dripped with accusation, guilt, and anger, and when she was mad she looked evil. At that moment, she was all of those things combined. She proceeded to tell me that Mrs. B. had seen Lee and I with our pants down and that we had been "touching ourselves."

The heat coming from my face was intense, as I now knew what Mrs. B. had seen and what my mother was talking about. I said nothing but was incredibly guilt-ridden. I was in big trouble. My mother told me how wrong this was and used the familiar words that I should "be ashamed of myself". She told me that I had to go to confession and tell the priest what I had been doing. She told me that I should never do this again and that I was grounded.

I think it was my reaction to hearing this that I find the most interesting of all.

I knew in that moment that I would never stop masturbating and that I would have to be more careful that I never got caught again!   Pretty amazing, isn't it?

I was already very reluctant about the church and about Catholicism itself. I went to church with my family every Sunday and went to confession like I was told, but thought that the nuns were cruel and that the priests were punitive. Around age three or four when I would go to church I would always sit next to my mother, I guess because I was the youngest. I would grab her hand to hold, not the other way around, meaning that my mother was not a naturally demonstrative person. Regardless, I would grab her hand and would press her long nails deeply into the space between my fingers. I would hold them there during the mass. It was as if I was a masochist or a saint and needed to inflict pain on myself in front of my family and God.

I think if someone had been paying attention they would have helped me at that age to resolve my masochistic tendencies, but that was not the case. I did confess to priest that I had been touching myself and I am sure he gave me some serious penance, but happily I do not remember that part because as I said, I knew that I would be doing it again and therefore the penance was all for naught!

By the time I was 11, I concocted a game that I would teach to my youngest brother called "Tickle Tush!" Yep, that's what I called it. He had been sharing a room with my oldest brother but by this time, my older brother was married and out of the house, leaving my little brother in a private room. My mother had taken up golf and would leave the house everyday during the summer months to play at least 18 holes. She would leave me in charge of my brother and we would have five or six hours to do our chores and play. Again, I don't remember the first time that we played "Tickle Tush" but it became a regular occurrence for us. He had bunk beds in his room and I would be on the bottom bunk and he would be on the top bunk where we would both be masturbating.

At the age of 10, I started having my period. I was at my full adult height of 5'2 ½ ", had breast buds and was in full-blown puberty. I did not know this at the time, but if a child has been sexually abused at an early age, (was I?) it is not uncommon for them to develop earlier than other children of the same age. However, it is also not uncommon for their secondary sex characteristics to be underdeveloped, hence my adolescent and adult flat-chested-ness.

This was true for me on one hand, my breasts never fully developed and my clitoris has always been enlarged. There was a time that I wondered if I had been born a hermaphrodite. And for those of you who are not familiar with what the definition of a hermaphrodite is: "a person having both male and female sex organs or other sexual characteristics."

I say this because my legs have been described as being very much like a male ballet dancers', with heavier, well-developed thighs and a rounded ass. Now in today's world, that is the new, hot body, but trust me, growing up in the 60's and 70's it was not popular at all! And having no breasts was also very tough for a girl like me, whose upper body was a size extra small while my lower body was a size 7 or 9! Just think of an upside down triangle. Or better yet, Nikki Minaj!

The women of that day were slender, with big breasts, usually implants, long blonde hair and most wore dresses. If I wanted to wear a dress, I would have to buy one that was large enough to go over my hips, which meant that the top of the dress would be way oversized and made me look ridiculous. So, I wore a lot of pants suits, which were actually fashionable.

I would have short hair when long hair was fashionable and long hair when short was chic! I was always ahead of the trends; a forerunner in fashion, but always alone in my category. I'll never forget going to Scottsdale with my sister in early 2000. I was wearing purple lipstick and black lip liner and she was mortified by all the negative attention I was getting. It would be years before this "Goth" style became popular. I bought my first pair of high-heeled gladiator sandals in 2003 and wore them nonstop for 10 years before they, too, became mainstream as well.

However, I think the biggest disappointment for me was when I got my first set of implants in 2001. It never dawned on me that small, natural, breasts would be the next new thing and am so bummed out that most of today's clothing is made for small-breasted women! An athletic female body with small breasts is the new body of choice. Sadly, once the skin on a woman's breast is stretched out for the implants she's kind of stuck with keeping them. It's something I never considered when I took that plunge!

JULY 5, 2014

I am a firm believer that illness is a result of unrecognized, unacknowledged, or trapped feelings in the body. But like so many people, I don't always remember my own beliefs when I get ill. This next story was a great learning experience for me.

I had spent Mother's Day with my Mom on May 11, 2014 in Buffalo and had seen a huge change in her mental status. My Dad had been dead for six years by this time and Mom had really gone down hill since.

My brother and his wife also lived in Buffalo and since my Mom was not doing as well living alone, the decision was made to sell our family home, where I had lived for 17 years, and move my mother into my brother's home.

My brother was still working full time but was also the full time caretaker of my sister-in-law, who had been suffering with Alzheimer's for the last 10 years. She was beginning to fail as well and it was obvious to us all that the end was near. She passed on June 27 and I went back to Buffalo to attend her celebration of life the first week of July.

It was during that second trip home that I had the sad awareness that my Mom, who now had Dementia as well as the beginning of Alzheimer's, no longer recognized me. I think you can imagine what that felt like. For me it was surreal. Sitting in front of me is the person who bore me, 59 years ago, but who now didn't know who I was.

This clearly hit me at a very deep level but was still somehow not in my conscious awareness based on what transpired after I returned home. I did not know it then but I had begun grieving my Mom's demise and on some level knew that she was not long for this world. She would be dead just three months later.

Even though I didn't consciously know what was happening, it appears that my body knew the difference. I began to have high blood pressure for the first time in my life and had to go to the E.R. one Sunday night after using one of the blood pressure machines at the local drug store.

It was on a Sunday and I hadn't felt well but couldn't put my finger on what could be wrong. I was on my way home from a friend's house to get ready to go to Oscar's Café in downtown Palm Springs for the weekly T-dance that was my "church", when I knew something was wrong. After thinking about all the possibilities, my intuition reminded me that I had not had my blood pressure checked in almost a year. Thinking logically rather then panicking , I decided to go the pharmacy to check it out.

Picture me; "shocked" when it read 160/105! As a Nurse, I knew that one reading was not enough so I decided to re-take it again after a few minutes but it was still elevated. I could see that this machine was not new and questioned its accuracy so I decided to run down to the next corner where a new Rite-Aide had opened. I was definitely feeling nervous, shaky, and scared. I was even more freaked out when the new reading was even higher at 170/110!

"This is so not like me", I thought. I don't have high blood pressure and I am not sick, overweight, or particularly nervous about anything, so why is my pressure so high?

And then panic and fear took over.

I immediately drove myself to the ER since it was after hours and the nearest Urgent Care had just closed. I went up to the front desk and told the triage nurse what was going on. I made sure she understood that I did not suffer from high blood pressure, that I had a headache and didn't feel well. I also told her that I did not have any other illness that would account for these symptoms.

She took my blood pressure reading and found it to be even more elevated which I am sure was part of my own response to being in the ER. Fear of the unknown! I was put on a gurney and immediately taken to a back room where they would run a number of tests to rule out stroke, heart attack, etc. Thankfully, they all came back negative.

At first I was quite panicky but then managed to get control of myself. Yes, I was in the E.R. alone, but God forbid if anything was seriously wrong this was the best place to be. I began to talk myself off the ledge of death and remembered all my self-help techniques for relaxation, which I knew was key.

I did my breathing exercises to try and relax. They monitored my vital signs and kept me hooked up to and EKG machine. This allowed me to see the effect of the relaxation exercises and after three hours my pressure came down on its own, without medication! I was discharged with instructions to see my primary Doctor the next day for follow-up, which I did. There, I was told that no one knew why my pressure had gone up and remained up, unless I had reached the age where people's blood pressure does go up naturally! This did not make sense to me because I am very athletic and do regular cardiovascular exercises and eat extremely well!

My hypertension lasted until the day my Mom died! It has never been elevated again! The body doesn't lie and the mind knows what it knows!

The only unfortunate part of this saga is that my insurance did not cover ER visits and I had to pay over $5,000.00 for a three-hour rest! Yuck!

AUGUST

AUGUST 16, 1921

There are so many big events that took place in my life during the months of August that it's a bit overwhelming as to where to start. But the one day that stands out the most is August 16, 1921 the day my mother was born. It is significant simply because she is my mother but even more unique in that August 16th is also a date shared by a "King" and a "Queen".

What do I mean, you ask? Well, Elvis Presley died on August 16, 1977 and Madonna was born on August 16, 1958, firmly putting that day on the map. But, as my Mom was born in 1921 it makes her the Grand Dame of August 16 and if I wasn't the dancer that I am and have the relationship with music that I do, I might not have ever realized the significance of the day that "the King of Rock and Roll died and the Queen was born!" If nothing else, it sure makes an interesting part of my story in my mind at least.

Synchronicity.

AUGUST 1972

I graduated from High School as a junior in August, 1972.

It was never my plan or intention to graduate a year early but as I had taken so many extra classes and been involved with so many groups I only needed four credits to graduate a year early. However, I did not know that until the day I went to sign up for summer school to take typing. The registrar was the person who mentioned to me that I only needed four credits to graduate. I had no idea that it was even an option and further did not know that I would make another life changing decision that day.

She told me which classes I needed to take but then told me that the classes were being offered simultaneously, making them impossible for me to attend. I can't explain how, but as I was looking at the schedule from my side of the table, which means that I was looking at it upside down, I somehow managed to see that there was another way to schedule those classes allowing me to take them at different times.

Amazingly, I spoke up for myself, which at the time was very uncharacteristic of me and showed her what I saw. I must have done it in the right way because she did not get defensive but instead congratulated me for seeing what she had missed! The fact that I spoke up for myself and corrected an adult was a paramount lesson for me at this time!

I was elated knowing that I was going to be able to get out of high school without getting pregnant, drug addicted, or committing suicide; all possibilities that I had toyed with at some point during my junior year!

High School was not my friend. I was so depressed in those days that it's amazing I ever even made it to school. But, I also knew that if I skipped school and got caught that the punishment at home would be far worse than any consequences the school could dole out!

I was very depressed throughout at least middle school and the three years I had already completed in high school. I was already anorexic and bulimic, had already had sex, and was about to become pregnant for the first time a few months later. I was a mess!

I had zero self-esteem, hated my body, and myself, and was extremely self abusive. I pulled out my hair, I bit my nails, and I masturbated 3-5 times or more a day, everyday. As a matter of fact I could not fall asleep at night unless I masturbated first. I hated my home life, I felt isolated most of the time and the number one goal in my life was to have a boyfriend who loved me!

I was very unhappy but felt a tiny modicum of hope that graduating early from high school would allow me to enter the work force sooner and be with real adults instead of all the "children" that I was surrounded by in school.

I graduated in mid-August and was asked by my parents what I would like for my graduation present. I wanted to go to Europe, but they made it clear that this was not an option for me. (Makes me wonder why they asked me what I wanted!) So, my next wish was to go visit my aunt who still lived in Whittier, CA. My grandmother had passed away in 1967, but my aunt and cousin still lived there.

My parents agreed to this request and a week later I took my first plane ride across country to Sunny California, my true home! We'll talk more about this in September.

AUGUST 1990

In August of 1990, I continued attending my Sex Addicts Anonymous (SAA) meetings; going almost every day. I was making new friends along the way. One of the friends was a girl named Tina. She was a lovely, sweet, sad, girl whom I now think was also lesbian, not that it makes any difference. We became close almost immediately. She was real and felt safe.

One warm summer day I was driving to a meeting in my Suzuki Jeep. It was hot and humid outside but my body temperature was very chilly. I did not know that I had a thyroid problem at that time, nor did I know that my regular body temperature was almost 2 degrees lower than the norm. My temperature was 96.8 not 98.6, making me cold most of the time regardless of the temperature outside.

The colder it was outside, the colder I was inside. Since that had been my norm for the majority of my life, I was in the habit of driving with one hand between my legs to keep warm. That was just me and I never thought much about it, well, until that day.

I was driving my jeep at the time and was wearing short shorts and a tube top. I had a chill all over my body even though it was most likely in the 80's or 90's and 90% humidity. I was listening to my cassette player and I'm sure was thinking about the meeting I was on my way to when I put my freezing cold hand between my legs. What happened next remains one of the biggest game changers in my life.

Out of nowhere, I suddenly had a flashback of a women's hand between my legs and started crying hysterically. It was the creepiest of feelings. It was not my own hand that I felt. I wasn't asleep. I wasn't dreaming. I was wide-awake! Now I should mention that I am a weeper and not a crier. I get teary-eyed watching the Hallmark channel but it's a rare moment in my life for me to cry out loud or to make noise.

But, that afternoon the tears and the gulps and the cries came at me from a very deep, dark place. I managed to keep driving while crying and made my way to the meeting. I was one of the first people there and rather than my typical, smiling self, I entered the room with my head down, crying, sniffling, and was so very sad as well as scared. WTF was going on!

Tina came into the room and saw me and ran right over to see what was wrong. I leapt into her arms and said,

"I think I just had my first memory of being sexually abused!"

She held me while I continued to cry, slowly regaining my composure. Once I could, I began to share with the group what had just happened. I got a lot of sympathy and encouragement but also knew that this was just the tip of the iceberg. I did not really appreciate or know that by clean and sober, removing all the chemicals from my brain and body had allowed past memories to fully emerge. I have come to appreciate this now.

Over the next few days, I became much quieter and more depressed and thoughtful. The days seemed longer and longer and the depression worsened. Around the 5th of August it seemed like all hell had broken loose. I was on my way to work where I was now the head of the Triage Department. I had my own office and kept my head down as I entered the building, avoiding eye contact, praying that no one would stop me before I made it into the office and could close my door where I knew I would burst into tears.

I went to my desk and sat down lowering my head onto the stack of mail waiting for me. I was crying and could not stop. It must have been 20 minutes or longer before I felt composed enough to lift my head. I felt like I had to get to work and figured the best place to start was with my mail.

Sitting on the top of the pile was a post card from Cottonwood Treatment Facility announcing their newest inpatient program for Sexual Abuse! I kid you not! There it was in black and white.

My universe was again looking out for me.

There was a number to call, which ironically was a direct line to their Triage Department. It was time to deal with this head on! Ready or not, here I come. Without missing a beat, I called the number and was instantly talking to a counselor about a patient; *me*! I explained my situation and told them who I was and where I worked. It didn't take long before the counselor said, "When would you like to be admitted?" At first I hemmed and hawed, saying I would need to talk to my supervisor and maybe I could come in around Sept 1st; definitely in my own denial about the urgency of the situation.

She reminded me that I was currently in crisis and now was the time to deal with this huge, life changing issue. She was telling me what I would have told someone calling our Triage line and I knew deep down it was what I needed to do.

After just a few minutes I came to my senses and said that she was right. She suggested I come in the next day, which I did. Yep, that was how it went down. I was now going to be a patient on a unit for people who had been sexually abused. I was scared and excited all at the same time. The first call I made was to my supervisor to request time off, the next was to my Mom.

Before Mom could ask me what or whom I was talking about, I volunteered that I thought that a babysitter might have sexually abused me. You see my mother had told me many times that when I was growing up I never made waves and I very rarely cried. But, a few years earlier, she told me that the only time I ever made a fuss was when a babysitter named Carol would come to sit for me. Mom said that I would scream and cry and tell my parents not to go. Again, back in those days people didn't think about abuse, sexual or otherwise, when it came to babysitters. There were no movies about these topics or even magazine articles, let alone the Internet, so parents were in the dark.

Since this type of behavior; "crying", was frowned upon in my family, I am sure I got one of those icy looks from my mother to "shut it down", which I did. We were born into a household where, "Children should be seen and not heard!" Tantrums were not tolerated nor were any other types of acting out behavior.

I honestly did not know who had sexually abused me but I knew something was wrong. I had a sneaking suspicion that it was either my paternal grandmother, who I stayed with whenever my parents went out of town, or the babysitter, whom I was terrified of, or maybe even someone else, but it didn't really matter, I just knew that something inappropriate had indeed happened based on all of my behaviors and that it had to do with sex.

Earlier I talked at great length about my history with masturbation, but have yet to share my history about men exposing themselves to me!

Oh yeah, it's true.

The first time that this happened to me, I was 14 years old. I was in Pier One in Buffalo, N.Y., minding my own business when I went down an aisle towards the back of the store. I was alone in the aisle until a man came around the corner wearing a tan raincoat. I didn't think much about it until he came towards me.

He opened his coat with one hand and in his other was his penis! He might have been the original "Flasher!"

I was totally flabbergasted and froze in my shoes, unable to move or to speak. I can't even remember who moved first. Did he turn and leave or did I? Either way, I had no idea what I was supposed to do. I remember feeling sick to my stomach, and I felt both embarrassed and ashamed. I never told anyone about what happened and just prayed that it would never happen again.

But, no such luck for this girl.

A year later, dealing with depression on a daily basis, I would do anything to leave my house and as I didn't yet have a car, I would ride my bike alone for hours. Initially, I would ride in my neighborhood but when I got bored would move onto the next neighborhood, and then the next until I was riding about 15 miles a day.

One day when I was about ½ hour from home I rode down a street, which happened to be near a middle school. I was riding past a car whose window was rolled down. There was a man sitting in the car and as I rode past I did the natural thing, I looked into his car and there he was masturbating!

Again, I was totally freaked out. He looked at me in the most disgusting way and I again felt sick to my stomach. I quickly did a U-turn rode as fast as I could to get away from him. I was fearful that he was going to come after me, but thankfully, he did not.

Another time, my cousin and I were going to go hang out at the airport. I'm not really sure why we were doing this, but this was in the early 70's and there were no security issues back in those days, so you could walk anywhere you wanted to, and airports were fun, bustling, places.

She was a few years older than me and had tried smoking cigarettes. Smoking in this era was considered very cool and sexy. We were going to buy cigarettes at the kiosk and pretend that we were waiting for a flight.

Now, I should mention that at this time in my life I must have been giving off a lot of sexual energy because I always had a lot of men interested in me. Many of these men sexually aroused me and I was constantly kissing them and getting both of us all worked up. It was no different on this particular day.

There was a very, very handsome, foreign looking man who caught my eye and vice versa. It didn't take long for our flirtation to escalate and he asked me to take a walk with him. Now my cousin was not too keen on this idea but I was and quickly convinced her that it was a harmless flirtation.

We headed down a hallway, flirting and toying with one another. It turns out that he was Italian and that his name was Sergio. That happened to be the name of my father's bosses son so it made it all that much more exciting. He felt somehow familiar and therefore somewhat safe.

Back in the 70's, telephone booths existed and clearly Sergio was no stranger to them. He had already kissed me several times by this point and as I said we were both turned on. At first when he suggested that we go into the phone booth to kiss it sounded like a good idea. I was hot and bothered and figured that it would be ok. I was still a virgin at this point, but I sure knew how to orgasm. I was hot and wet and when he pressed himself up against me it felt great.

He put my hand on his penis and it was big and hard. I had done a lot of this heavy petting before so it just felt good. But, when he put his hands down my pants and stuck his fingers into my wet vagina it was way too much for me. I mean I didn't even know this man and it was daylight and we were in the middle of the airport.

My age was showing and I couldn't deal with my own feelings, so I grabbed his hand, pulled it out of my pants and ran back to my cousin, who was anxiously awaiting my return. We left the airport moments later and vowed to never speak of what happened again. Honestly, I think this is the first time that I ever have mentioned it outside of my own head!

Then on a trip to Bermuda around 1978 while taking a short cut to the beach off the beaten track, I ran into a native man who was masturbating in the sand dunes.

Fast forward to 1982 when I lived in Chicago and used to jog every day. I was on my way back home when I passed an alleyway where a man stood in the shadows masturbating.

One of the last times was when I worked in Chicago for the Visiting Nurse Association. I was in my car driving from one patient's house to another when the signal turned red so I stopped my car. As I was sitting at the light looking around I happened to look up at an open window. In the window was a man who was masturbating. He looked right at me and smiled in that weird, creepy way that people do when they are doing something wrong. I barely waited for the light to change before speeding off to get as far away from him as I could. Again, WTF? What is wrong with me?

What message was I sending out? Why was this happening to me over and over again? What did it mean?

I was so afraid to tell anyone about these encounters because I was sure that it meant that I was a sick person and that was why *I* was attracting all these so called perverts! Right?" I think my bigger fear was that it meant that *I* was a pervert; to be honest, I did masturbate all the time, didn't I?

Was this my universe telling me I was sick?

I finally mustered up the courage to mention one or two of these occurrences to a girl that I knew, but she had never had anything like that happen to her, so I quickly nixed the subject and never broached it with anyone again!

So now, knowing all this history, its back to the Cottonwood Inpatient Treatment Facility.

The program consisted of group, individual, and art therapies all attempting to uncover and discover what had happened to get me admitted here. I continued to believe that it was the babysitter who had done something to me and for the first two weeks focused on what that must have been like. It seemed to fit based on my mother's description of my behavior but it turns out that I had another memory while I was there and this one made a lot more sense to me.

I started remembering a big red leather chair that was in my parent's bedroom. At first I could just see the chair, something I hadn't thought about in years.

But then I started having memories of the large mirror that hung over my mother's dresser in their bedroom. Now this mirror was very significant to me because it was in front of this mirror that I would masturbate whenever my parents were out of the house. I had a mirror over my own dresser but somehow found it necessary to go into their room to take care of myself sexually. I did this thousands of times while living in their house.

I am going to tell you something else that is very difficult to admit out loud. If I was in my bedroom and felt the urge to masturbate, I would stand in front of my dresser (again, notice this mirror pattern) to do so. Typically, my bedroom door would be open by just a crack. Through this crack I had a perfect view of my parents closet. My Dad had a habit of getting dressed in his closet after showering in the hall bathroom that we all shared.

Through this crack, I could see him in his boxer shorts and socks while he was picking out his clothes. The hard and shameful part to admit is that is that I used to masturbate to him and fantasize about him in order to orgasm. I felt a rush of energy and a ton of guilt all at the same time.

What kind of a freak was I? Who masturbates to their father? What was wrong with me?

During these same years my father and I had a true love/hate relationship. I was both afraid of him as well as hating him but I also wanted his approval. So much of this now makes sense to me but it has taken years for me to forgive myself for all these apparently inconsistent behaviors. These conflicting behaviors are key components in anorexic females who tend to be approval seekers and will do almost anything to attain that approval. When I began to have the flashbacks of this mirror in their bedroom it was both relieving and frightening.

Here's what I saw:

My father, who was totally naked, is standing in front of the mirror holding me (a tiny baby) against his torso. I'm facing forward, my back against his stomach. My legs are on both sides of his penis, which was erect, and he's moving my legs back and forth in constant motion like one would do if they were giving someone a hand-job.

This would make my father the first person in my life that had taken advantage of me from behind, which sets up a pattern that repeats itself later in my life.

As a teenager I had very severe acne on my back, which makes me wonder if I was trying to push out putrid memories from this experience. No telling but who can really say for sure?

This memory made sense to me for the following reasons:

I knew I was as virgin the first time I had sex because I bled and it hurt like crazy which meant that my Dad had not penetrated me. All of my life my orgasms have been clitoral and not vaginal which would make sense if you consider that my Dad's penis was stimulating my "baby" clitoris each and every time that he moved my legs back and forth. This friction felt incredible and was a feeling I obviously wanted to re-create as often as I could. But somewhere down the road I also knew that it was taboo and judged *myself* as bad.

Unconsciously, I was returning to the scene of the crime standing in front of that mirror in their bedroom to masturbate. Even watching my Dad through the door in his bedroom made sense in that the abuse took place in that same room.

Puberty is the natural time that orgasms and our secondary sex characteristics get developed unless, as in my case, they are turned on prematurely. This is why I believe I was so fixated on masturbation and having orgasms. I was also very aware of my own sexual attractiveness to men of all ages.

But, this was in 1990 and we were all still in the dark ages regarding sexual abuse. I had never seen a Television program that showed a scene like this, nor have I ever read about a sexual abuse case like this. Not then, let alone now, so I trusted this memory.

In my attempt to understand how this may have come about, I have done a lot of thinking, talking and of course have had years of therapy, too. Here are some of the beliefs that I have come to accept.

My parents were not overtly sexual people to my childhood eyes; my mother did not dress provocatively and neither one of them were touchy-feely people or huggers. They would superficially kiss one another on birthdays, anniversaries, and holidays. Way before my mother went into menopause I found a box of Trojans in my Dad's nightstand. It remained full and had expired years earlier, making me think that my parents were not having sex of any kind. They also slept with their bedroom door open so I'm pretty certain that I am correct in my beliefs.

Growing up in Buffalo we were all skiers and my dad and uncle built a ski chalet that had four bedrooms. Between all the kids, this meant that there were not enough bedrooms to go around. Being the youngest at the time, I slept in my parent's bedroom.

I always had a lot of anxiety when it came to bedtime and any light coming into the room or noise like people talking or the TV kept me awake. If I were awake when they came to bed, they would yell at me and tell me to go to sleep. Therefore, I learned at an early age to pretend I was asleep when my parents made their way upstairs after the 11:00pm news. Evidently, there were a number of occasions where my Dad would attempt to be sexual with my Mom but she would turn him down, because I would hear her say, "Stop it Guido, and go to sleep!"

Maybe she knew I wasn't asleep, maybe she was frigid, or maybe she just wasn't interested. Or, perhaps she was angry with him for his bullying behavior and frugal ways. Whatever the reason, she was not available to him physically or sexually. It makes me wonder if that was what was happening during my first year of life as well.

If my Mom had been experiencing post-partum depression she would not have any interest in sex. It is also likely that she had guilt feelings about not being able to hold me and perhaps became withholding with him as a way to deal with her own guilt. My mother also told me that because of her illness, my dad had had to hold and comfort me as a baby. This, after a long day's work, must have been an imposition that he could have resented. After all, in an Italian home, caretaking of the children would not have fallen on the father.

I will never know what precipitated my Dad's need to use me for a sex tool, but can certainly understand that it happened and more importantly believe my memories.

As a matter of fact, what happened during family week at the Cottonwood Facility helped me understand so much of my behavior that I must share it with you now.

The last week of treatment in many 30-day rehab facilities usually involves family week; a week where the people of your choosing are invited to participate in classes and groups to help them understand what their loved one has gone through. It is open to anyone that the patient feels is important to his or her full recovery. In the case of sexual abuse the only people that the week is not open to is to an abuser, in this case my dad. However, when the plans were made for my parents to attend, I had not yet had the memories of this abuse, so he was invited along with my mom.

The counselors at Cottonwood approached me to tell me that my Dad was not going to be able to participate because he was now being identified as the transgressor and I instantly became mortified and panicked. Who was going to tell him this and when? I knew that I would be in trouble. This is my pattern. I feel guilty when I believe things go wrong.

I was then living in Georgia and they were in New York State. They had to purchase plane tickets and, knowing them, I knew they would be non-refundable. You can see how my mind works, can't you? I am already taking responsibility for my Dad's rage at losing money let alone his rage for being accused of being an abuser!

My anxiety soared and then lessened slightly when the counselor's said it was their role to tell my Dad that he couldn't participate.

Here's how it went down instead.

My parents were sent the schedule of the week's activities and rules.

Rule #1 firmly stated that all participants must be at the facility by 9:00am Monday morning, no exceptions!

Now my Dad, who had just retired from his job after 45 years was going to be a consultant. His first gig happened to be at 8:00am Monday morning! His consultant fees were close to $100 an hour, far exceeding his normal hourly wage. He planned to go to the meeting and then run to airport to catch a 9:30am plane and be in Georgia by 11:30am. My mother, however was to arrive the night before, so she would be on time.

My Dad arrived at Cottonwood around noon according to the counselor who shared the story with me later that same day. She said that he walked in and introduced himself, identified me as the patient and asked where he should go. He was told that the sessions had begun at 9:00am and that he was too late to join in.

He misunderstood the information and asked what time he should be back the next morning. And although I wasn't present when he was told that he would not be allowed to participate at all, I could clearly see in my mind, the look on his face.

He stammered, " What? I've come all this way to be here for my daughter, what in the world are you talking about?"

He was reminded of the rules that stated that all family members must be present by 9:00am on Monday morning with no exceptions. He said he could not help being late and explained that he had been at work. The counselor said that it was a shame that he had made the choice to work, rather than be there for his daughter, but the rules were solid and they made no exceptions, period.

I remember thinking that I wished I had been there to see this, internally realizing that this was the first time that my Dad had ever been told "No."

I was secretly pleased that someone had finally stood up to him!

They relayed that he had tried to coerce them three or four times before they had to ask him to leave. I was told that his face had been beat red and he looked totally out of control. But, he was being refused admission based on time, not for being an abuser! So, I would still have to confront him as part of my own recovery.

My mother in the meantime was attending classes and groups during the day and was left to deal with my father's disgust at the program rules at night.

What happened Monday morning with my Mom was also pretty awful. We were allowed to greet our family members first as group and then one-on-one. Mom and I superficially hugged one another and then went into a room to talk. My Mom asked me exactly why she was here and what I was doing in this treatment program.

With my stomach in my throat, I remember choosing my words very carefully and said, "I'm here because I was sexually abused as a child!" She looked at me with a combination of fear, anger, and disgust but mostly with anger as she said; "You better be very careful with what you are about to say, do you understand?" She gave me her raised eyebrow look, the one that had controlled my emotional responses for the majority of my life. Later, I would come to see the synchronicity of this same look in my relationship with Stew. A raised eyebrow, whether from a mother or a lover, triggers strong emotions in me to this day.

I remember feeling sick to my stomach and remember how freezing cold my whole body felt. She was basically telling me that she did not want to know my truth.

I saw my Dad for the first time that Monday afternoon when he had come to fetch Mom after class. He was still so enraged that he could barely look at me and told me how screwed up the place was for not letting him participate.

I was so uncomfortable. I could not make eye contact with him. I really didn't know what to say, let alone how to speak the truth.

I did not see either of them again until week's end when some very significant things happened.

My oldest brother called me to tell me that my Dad, who had been stuck in a hotel room all week, angry and bored out of his mind had called him and admitted to him that, a **boy in his neighborhood had sexually abused him** when he was 10 years old!

WOW! Are you kidding me? This was huge!

He said that my Dad had never told anyone about this until now. That was a huge relief for me because it is a well-known fact that abusers have often been abused. It made me think many things about my Dad. I felt empathy, I felt sad, I felt hurt, I felt angry but the important thing is that I felt!

This was never discussed again and of course my Dad never went to therapy to deal with his own feelings.

It was now the final day of family week and after having had no contact with our family member, we were re-united with them for a final activity before saying goodbye. All of the patients were seated at tables in a large, cold, room and the family members were called in to join us. They were given the instruction to stand behind us.

The family members had been given a sheet of paper that listed 20 things that they could say to us. They were asked to choose the one that was closest to how they felt about said person. The list was both specific as well as general from 'I love you' to 'you are a child of God.' The family member was told to place their hands on our shoulders, bend down and repeat the line into our ear.

When my Mom put her hands on my shoulders, they were freezing cold and her touch was so stiff that I actually felt as if she were an Eagle and that her fingers were talons. I automatically stiffened up while I awaited her words, hoping that they would be warm enough to take the cold, impersonal feeling away.

We, too, had also been provided with the list and I had chosen a statement that was both personal and loving. It was so much what I wanted to hear from my Mom. But, it was not to be and I was totally shocked when she said to me,

"You are a child of God and he loves you!"

WHAT? REALLY? Are you kidding me?

But, there it was folks, this was all I was going to get.

On one hand I was super hurt and on the other I already knew the score. My mother was not comfortable with anyone's feelings, especially not her own. I was pretty numb by this time and basically wanted the whole thing to be over with.

My child-like fantasy that my mother would become this warm and fuzzy person was dead! But, this was not the end. A few minutes later as things were winding up, I heard my name being called over the loud speaker with the instructions to come to a room on the first floor.

Oh my God, I thought, what now? Could it get any worse?

I was scared, nervous and mortified as I walked to the room and opened the door where I saw all of the counselors sitting in a big circle. I feared that they were going to tell me that I was crazy or something just as bad. I'm sure the look on my face said it all because the leader of the group assured me that I was not in trouble and invited me to come in and take a seat, which I did.
In a million years I could not have predicted what they were going to tell me.

The leader said, "In this room of 20 or more therapists is about 100 years of experience. We wanted you to know that we had never met a *more defended* person than *your mother*.

They went on to tell me that they tried every skill they had to help her lower her defenses; to help her see what had really been going on at our house. Each and every time as she was approaching the breaking point, she would shut down and deny everything that she had almost been ready to accept!

Further they said that they felt that they owned it to me to tell me that whatever it was that I had hoped to get from my mother was never going to happen. And, in order for me to fully recover, I needed to realize that she was incapable of giving me what I needed and that I would be better off relying on my own internal resources and strengths. They told me to believe in myself, trust my instincts, and to get on with my life.

This was an incredible gift!

They also told me that they believed in me and could see how strong I was to have survived my mother's emotional limitations. They told me that I was a very strong person and would go far. They then reminded me of the anger and rage that they had seen in my father and imagined how controlling he was as a parent. They helped me see that I was better off separating myself from them and moving on alone, to which I agreed.

Trust me when I tell you that I was blown away as well as relieved and appreciative of their comments, love and encouragement. It was the last thing I could have imagined!

We had one last meeting after that and this time it was with both of my parents. I had chosen to distance myself from my parents for a minimum of a year in order to heal and was going to have to tell them that in this meeting. I will never forget not only what my father said to me, but how he said it, as well.

"So if your grandmother dies, you don't want us to contact you?" my father said snidely.

Since I had been forewarned that my parents would try to guilt me into conceding to their wishes, I just shook my head and said, "Yes", barely able to look him in the eye. It was one of the hardest conversations I have ever had. But, I did it! We said our superficial good-byes and they left!

I was discharged a few days later.

SEPTEMBER

SEPTEMBER 2, 1991

I was discharged from Cottonwood Treatment Center on September 2, 1991, also known as Labor Day here in the U.S.

This particular date is so meaningful in my life because it was not only my discharge date but it was also the day that Stew's second wife was killed in 1999. Had this accident never occurred, I would not have married Stew and might not have ever come to Palm Springs where I would become my authentic self. In my heart of hearts I believe in destiny so perhaps it's not worth questioning any further.

I was discharged and headed home feeling very shaky. I didn't know what to expect of my life or myself. First of all, it felt like my vision had changed. By this I mean when I opened the front door to my house I noticed how different everything looked. It was like I was Alice in Wonderland. My furniture looked huge while the rooms seemed small. It was a bit like my first and only acid trip.

My hearing was more acute and as a matter of fact all of my senses were on hyper-drive. Since it was the holiday weekend I still had one more day to re-group before returning to work and I used the time to try to calm myself down, but I could tell I had changed.

What I was not prepared for was the strength of my inner voice. I made it through Labor Day weekend. It was now Tuesday and I was driving to work feeling really unsettled. I pulled into the hospital parking lot and parked my car. I sat there for a few minutes before forcing myself to get out of the car. As I was walking up to the front door I heard this voice saying; "Don't go in there!"

At first I thought maybe I was really crazy until I realized that I actually did NOT want to go in there. I felt sick to my stomach and thought I was going to throw up. I stopped dead in my tracks and stood there forcing myself to take a few deep breaths to try to calm myself down.

Because so much of the inpatient program had revolved around trusting yourself, honoring your inner child and being able to hear yourself, I said to myself out loud, "I hear you and I honor what you are feeling." This gave me the courage to know that I no longer wanted to work in this environment and knew that I was at a crossroad. I knew I was going to quit my job!

But, how I was going to do this was the hard part, or so I thought in the moment.

When I entered the building the reception staff greeted me warmly. I said my "hellos" before making my way to my office. I wasn't in there five minutes when my phone rang. I quickly answered and heard the one voice I hated; a guy whom I had no respect for and whom I greatly disliked. He was gloating when he told me that he needed to see me ASAP. He asked if I had heard that the hospital had gone through some administrative changes over the five weeks that I had been gone. I answered yes but I cringed when he said that he was now the new administrator! Great, I thought, the one person I can't stand is now my new boss. He said he was in his office and that *he* would see *me* now!

So, off I went. I sat in the seat facing his desk, avoiding eye contact for fear that my disgust would be too easily seen and felt and awaited my sentencing. He droned on for a few minutes and I'm not even sure I was listening to him because the voice in my head kept saying; "get out now!" I only became aware of it as he was going over my options. The first was to take a demotion and the second was to quit and receive 6 weeks severance pay! It took me about two seconds to blurt out; "I'll take the severance pay!"

The next thing I knew, I was in my office packing up my personal belongings, collecting my check and was back in my car in the parking lot. It was now 9:45am and I was an unemployed Nurse for the first time in my life. It was now time for me to help myself and begin to nurse *myself* back to my life and stop taking care of other people.

I was scared shitless because I had a mortgage payment due monthly as well as a car payment and I had no one to help me but myself. I somehow found the strength to sign up for a graphic arts class where I would learn how to make my own business cards. I had always had a real knack for interior design and fashion and thought it was time to take a break from nursing and use some of my other God-given talents.

I started a business to help people re-design their homes using what they had on hand. I called myself an *alteránt,* a Latin word used back in the 1600's meaning "one who alters". I put an ad in the local penny saver and, low and behold, got a few jobs. It was a very frightening time but it was also a time for me to move ahead in my life.

I finally mustered up the courage to write my Dad a letter confronting him with his abuse of me. I'm sure that I wrote many copies before choosing exactly the one that I finally sent. I put the letter into an envelope, which said Personal and Confidential, then sealed it in another one, which I addressed to him.

I knew my parents rather well and believed that my Mom would not open the letter but also prayed that I was right. I had also just received a bill from the treatment facility saying that I owed them $21,000.00! I was mortified because I thought that my health insurance would pay the majority of it, but was mistaken and was now devastated that I had this huge debt and just quit my well paying job.

Up until this point I had not asked my parents for any help. They had paid for my schooling at both B.G.H. as well as Emory but I had worked while I was in school and paid for all my own expenses. I don't mean to sound ungrateful or unappreciative but I'd been on my own for 11 years and had never asked for a dime let alone a loan.

My Dad did respond to my letter, denying everything, of course, and wrote to me that he thought I had confused him for my childhood B.F.F's father who we knew had sexually abused her. He wrote that he had recently watched an episode of Law and Order where a girl had been admitted to an inpatient unit and her therapists had convinced her that she had been sexually abused to get more money out of the insurance company. I wrote back that this was not the case for me and proudly told him that whether he believed me or not, I believed *me*!

I remember hugging myself very tightly while saying out loud to my inner child that I believed and trusted *my* feelings, which was huge step for me. I then sent a copy of the hospital bill to him and said that I thought he owed me this much! He agreed to pay it but then sent me a letter saying that this amount would be deducted from any inheritance that I might receive. For the record, he did not include that note in his will, for which I am grateful.

I believe that this was his passive-aggressive attempt at taking responsibility. I will never know for certain but I will tell you that when he died we had resolved our differences and had come to love and respect one another on a different level.

September 2, 2000

Stew, the bodybuilder, and I had planned a trip to Durango, Colorado to commemorate the trip that he and his second wife had been on when she was accidently killed. They had been on their way to a big motorcycle rally in Durango when Stew lost control of the bike. He managed to stop his motorcycle from falling over and had pulled onto the side of the road to re-group. A few minutes later, his son from his first marriage who was riding with them, came around the same corner. He also lost control of his bike and careened into the back of his dad's motorcycle and his step-mom killing her instantly! Yes, it's true and so very tragic.

I had met the two of them when they moved from Houston, Texas to Santa Fe, New Mexico earlier that year. I had been blown away by their physiques and their relationship and hired them to train me in May. She was now dead and Stew and I were not only dating but had gotten engaged as well. I had only had one boyfriend in the past that drove a motorcycle and as much as I thought they were somewhat cool, was not really into the lifestyle. But, being the "good obedient girl" that I was at the time; I agreed to accompany him on this memorial trip.

We packed the bike and off we went. I have to admit that I was both nervous and excited. We would be on the same Harley that she had been killed on and I was now sitting in her seat! You can only imagine what that felt like and what I was thinking about the entire time.

We happily made the 212-mile journey without a hitch and checked into a beautiful downtown Durango hotel. After dinner we decided to go shopping and this is when I spotted the most unusual wooden sculpture. This one happened to be carved, not in Poland, but instead in Bali, which is ironically where Stew and his wife had originally planned to get married.

The sculpture was made from one piece of wood, in this case a root from a palm tree. How ironic that we would end up moving to the home of Palm Trees; Palm Springs! Could this be another sign?

We were walking down the street when I noticed the sculpture in the front window and it immediately caught my attention. I stopped for just a minute to look up at it and then started to move onward when I felt an energy pulling me back to it. I have to say that I had never felt anything like this before, well actually, maybe I had.

Do you recall the incident with the umbrella when I was getting ready to walk down the aisle at my first wedding? This energy was even stronger than that. This time, I had been thrown back to the store window. Stew, who noticed my obvious reaction, asked if I wanted to go in to take a look at it. I said, "Yes, I think that would be a good idea!" I felt like I didn't have any other choice.

We went in and boy, did I look. I was immediately drawn to the two figures, a man and a woman. They were kneeling next to one another, the man on the right and the woman on the left, just the way that I was taught about the two sides of our bodies. But, what is even more significant, is when I realized that the artist had carved muscles on both figures, which I thought was fascinating because I was now a woman with muscles. I knew I had never seen anything like that before and got closer to it to take a better look. The figures looked so much like Stew and me it was uncanny.

Stew asked me if I would like to have it, and this really threw me for a loop. The sculpture was $650 and to me that was a lot of money. I had not been "Daddy's little Princess" and had never been showered with gifts by any male. As a matter of fact, I had always been the breadwinner in every relationship I had been in up to this time. The thought of a man offering to buy me what I considered to be an expensive gift for no other reason than I liked it was totally amazing and a bit overwhelming.

I very meekly said, "Yes." And he bought it for me and had it shipped to our home in Santa Fe. All was good until the sculpture arrived and I had a chance to really look it over.

I mentioned that the figures were kneeling next to each other and when I examined the juxtaposition of their body parts I realized that the sculptor had placed the right arm and hand of both people onto their crotch area. Now I have told you that my first memory of being sexually abused happened when I had placed my cold hand between my legs while driving my jeep. So this was both unique and weird, don't you agree?

Even odder was that fact that the woman had a large wooden knot on her right buttock. I say that because when I was 10 years old I was in an accident that required a skin graft. The surgeon had taken a square patch of skin off on my right buttock to use on my left leg. Okay, that seems a bit coincidental but the shape of the knot just so happens to be the exact shape of the burn on my leg, which is not square at all! A number of years ago, I put a piece of tracing paper on the knot on the woman's buttock and then cut it out just to see if it was the same shape as my burn. I kid you not when I tell you that the paper fits my scar perfectly!

I'd love to tell you that this is the end of the story surrounding this wooden sculpture but it is not. Fast forward to 2006, when Stew and I re-located to Palm Springs after my epiphany at the White Party. It was at the end of our move-in day and we were in the garage sorting out boxes. We had been moving all day long and we were ready for this day to end. A friend was helping us out and the three of us were a bit slap-happy.

The lot we chose in the Mesa was the last remaining 1/5-acre of the Gillette estate and was very hilly. We had to spend a ton of money to cut out a flat spot for the house and had to build ten steps to get from the driveway up to the house. According to code, we also had to install an outside door at the top of the stairs because we had a pool in our courtyard. We had propped the door open so that we could carry furniture and boxes in without having to stop each time to re-open the door.

Earlier in the day, I had gently carried my 20-pound sculpture up the stairs and placed it in the niche outside that we had built to showcase it. We had a main house as well as a casita and for some reason, the glass guys had trouble cutting the bathroom mirror for the casita and had to make a new one. The old one just so happened to fit perfectly in the niche, so when I sat the sculpture in the niche, I noticed that the mirror allowed you to see the back of it as well as the front, making for a very pretty picture.

While we were in the garage, we heard the sound of the wind, which would normally not be a big deal. We had been told numerous times how much we would enjoy living in south Palm Springs because there was never any wind, so this definitely got our attention. Out of nowhere the wind became gusty and wild. The trees were all shaking and the dirt and sand were flying. Suddenly, the next sound we heard was three things: a slam, a smash, and a crash! We all looked up at one another and the guys simultaneously said; " What was that?"

Without missing a beat I said; "The door slammed, the sculpture fell, and the mirror broke!"

As we walked out of the garage, we looked up to the top of the stairs to see the door closed. We walked up the stairs and opened the door to see the sculpture face-first on the patio surrounded by the broken mirror. My heart sank in my chest and there was an eerie and uncomfortable moment before I found myself saying; "This is either a very good sign or a very bad one." I somehow knew that it was the latter and not the former. The guys were in total shock and disbelief and did not, or could not, say a word.

I bent down to retrieve the sculpture to see if it was damaged and was even more blown away with what I found. The male took the brunt of the damage since he was taller than the female. There was an indentation on what would be his forehead. Now this alone would be unfortunate because it had damaged the sculpture but that is not what makes it so freaky. Stew had been born with a wine-spot birthmark on the center of his forehead (think Gorbachev). For some reason it never bothered him enough to have it removed. However about 20 years ago one of his best friends, the surgeon who gave me my first boob job, volunteered to remove the birthmark. This had left a scar in the middle of his forehead and now the sculpture had the same scar! Go figure! What does it all mean? Is this art imitating life and not the other way around? I am not sure but I of course have many thoughts on the topic.

The final note is that the next morning when we woke up, we found a dead bird in our swimming pool! I also felt that this was not a positive sign for our new house and ultimately, our marriage. By the way, this is not an Alfred Hitchcock episode or upcoming movie! But, it is my life!

SEPTEMBER 2, 2009

Another freaky thing happened on another Sept 2nd, but this time in 2009. It was about our dog, Max. Stew had Max, a Maltese from his first marriage. Max was Stew's best friend and he was not afraid to show it. I must confess that Max and I did not see eye to eye and had a tumultuous relationship at best! Max had gone thru Stew's first divorce, then met and lived with Stew's second wife until her death in 1999, which is when I entered the picture.

Perhaps as a dog, Max decided that I was one wife too many, leaving him disinterested at best. I'm not an animal person since I had never grown up around them, so I really did not know how to respond to Max as I should have. I picked up on his ambivalence to me early on. He did not seem to want to share Stew with me, and vice versa. Stew on the other hand made it very clear that he liked animals more then people. So I knew I was never going to be running with the Big Dogs.

I was also just needy enough for attention, any attention, something that I had only gotten in the past if I was doing something wrong. Talk about negative reinforcement! But Stew was the first man who ever saw me, heard me, and let me talk. He saw who I could become and encouraged that part of me to come to the surface. Regardless of the reasons, Max and I both left one another alone and let Stew be the main human in his life.

Max had been there for Stew when his second wife died and felt his pain, licked his tears, and comforted him in a way that no human could. It was obvious to anyone that knew Stew that he embodies the characteristics of a modern day St. Francis. All types of animal loved him, and he them. I really didn't have much of a chance at all to bond with Max unless perhaps if I had been St. Clare. In my heart I believed that Max and Stew had spent many lifetimes together. I think that in another life, Max was Stew's horse and best friend. But, that's just me!

Stew and Max were two peas in a pod and appeared to be attached at the hip. At night Stew and Max had this very cute ritual. Stew would say goodnight, put his head on the pillow while turning onto his left side. Max would then climb between us, snuggle his back up to Stew's back and simultaneously put his head on Stew's pillow. At the same moment, they would inhale, make a big sigh and fall asleep. Perhaps a more accurate description is that they were attached at the back!

If Stew had a quick errand to run when we were out, he would leave Max and me in the car with the A/C running. The second he left the car; Max would put his paws up on the dashboard and would not move until Stew returned to the car. He would make a noise that sounded like a baby crying for its parent to return. If I made any attempt to comfort him, he would stiffen his body and basically ignore me. Being the overly sensitive person that I was, it hurt my feelings and I too would retreat from him. It sounds rather crazy now and I'm a bit embarrassed to admit it, but it's the truth.

Once we moved to Palm Springs, Stew continued to have work in Santa Fe and would travel back for business. Max would mope around the house once Stew left and would basically ignore me and me him. I know it must sound childish and perhaps it was, but to be totally ignored by another, animal or otherwise, got to me. I'm sure it says way more about my insecurities and inadequacies than anything else, but being ignored does get old and it hurts.

In 2009, when Stew left late in August, Max suddenly stayed very close to me and wouldn't leave my side. Wow, what was going on? I was so excited, thinking that he had finally come to accept me and mentioned this behavioral change to my B.F.F. Eric who was visiting. He'd been around Max and me many times and agreed that this was a huge change. We both thought it was good news.

Max stayed like this for the next three days. He seemed calm and collected and never in a million years did I surmise that anything was wrong. That is until Stew came home.

The normal routine for would be for Stew to pull into the driveway and Max would hear the car long before Stew would ascend the ten stairs in front of our house. Stew would come through the solid wood door and Max would dance around and bark, showing his joy that his master was finally home!

On this particular day, Max only lifted up his head from where he was lying, obviously realizing that Stew was home and then just put his head down and stayed where he was. I went to greet Stew and as we were hugging, he asked me about Max. I proudly said, "He's laying down in the bedroom. He's been so good; I think that he and I finally bonded on this trip!"

Stew immediately called out to him, expecting him to come racing out the door but Max did not budge. Stew went into the bedroom to see him, took one look at him and said, "I think he's sick."

He touched his nose, which evidently was very warm and indicative of illness, which I did not know. "How long has he been like this?" he asked me and I said; "Since yesterday, when he vomited and he hasn't eaten much today!" Max occasionally did vomit so I didn't think much of it until Stew asked about the color of the vomit.

I said it had been yellow, again, not knowing its importance. Stew immediately said that he was going to take him to the vet.
I felt terrible. Had my need to be accepted by Max overshadowed the fact that he had been ill? I had never seen nor been around a sick pet, so I didn't know what to look for. Max had never been sick before so I had no reason to think that he was now. But, I still felt incredibly guilty.

As it turns out Max had hepatitis, which evidently is very rare in dogs. His liver enzymes were through the roof, so much so, that he was admitted to the animal I.C.U., where he stayed for 7 days, running up a $7,000.00 bill!

Max totally recovered even after we were told that he wouldn't make it. The craziest thing of all is that he stayed completely well for exactly nine months, until he got sick for the final time. On June 2, 2010 he took ill again. This just happened to be Stew's Dad's birthday and four days later, which was Stew's sister's birthday, we had to put him down.

So many anniversary days, so many coincidences; but are they?

The most unbelievable thing happened during Max's last nine months. Max and I finally bonded. We literally became best friends and companions. I don't know why or how this came to be, but it did and I am so grateful. I loved Max and Max loved me. I cried the day we put him down and I am crying now just writing this. But there is another amazing piece to this saga that has to do with Max's spirit and the spirits that now come to me on a regular basis. I don't know about you but I never believed in ghosts or spirits and perhaps many of you don't either. However, the first time that one came to me while I was asleep it was preceded by a visit from Max.

I was sleeping on my back when I felt the bed move the way it does when a small pet jumps up onto the mattress. I thought nothing of it and even less when Max came up and laid on my chest. I started to pet him the way that I had those last nine months until I woke up enough to remember that Max was gone!

Holy Shit! My eyes sprung open and standing at the foot of the bed was an apparition. My heart was beating a mile a minute. I did not recognize the spirit but I know what I saw. This began to happen to me over and over again and each time, prior to the spirit's arrival, *my Max* comes to me in the same way to alert me as to what was coming next.

Initially, I was fearful of the encounters and for years couldn't even say a word out loud. Now I realize that they are peaceful spirits and I am able to speak to them and ask them what they want of me. So, I take this moment to thank Max for being my animal spirit guide and am totally grateful that we were able to become friends.

SEPTEMBER 19, 2012

Stew and I had separated in July of 2012 as our unresolved issues continued. Being on my own meant that I now had new responsibilities and Netflix was one of them.

They had contacted me to ask if I wanted to continue with their service. Stew had always been in charge of our account so I needed to decide if I would or could benefit from their service and began to peruse the movies that they offered.

I was obviously meant to see one title in particular; "The Way."
This movie affected me so greatly that I cried all the way through it. It's a movie that follows four very different individuals who are walking through the Pyrenees Mountains in northern Spain on a Pilgrimage called the Camino de Santiago. It's like a new age version of the Wizard of Oz.

The main character reminded me of a combination of my Dad and Stew so, as soon as I finished watching it, I sent Stew a text recommending it to him. It would not be until January of 2013 that he watched it and that is how we ended up walking the Camino ourselves in May of 2013.

SEPTEMBER 1, 2005

Stews' and my first gay cruise coincided with the days Katrina was demolishing New Orleans in early September 2005. I was so excited to be flying overseas to join 2,000 gay men aboard a huge ocean liner on my first Atlantis cruise. I had never been on a cruise before and couldn't wait for the experience. I was not disappointed and have talked in great detail about the men's reactions to Stew and me earlier!

We were an anomaly but ended up being the talk of the cruise. I mentioned that many of those same men are my dear friends today and the experience was one of the most memorable of my life, all for the best of reasons. I loved traveling to the French and Italian Rivieras, Rome, Mykonos, Vesuvius, and Pompeii. I also loved spending a few days post cruise in beautiful Barcelona, one of my favorite cities.

In September 2001, Stew and I attended our first Olympia, the main event in the Bodybuilding world. We were so psyched to watch the top contenders in the world compete on stage at the Mandalay Bay in Las Vegas! By this time I had already competed in three amateur shows and knew the drill, so we used this opportunity to get in contest shape and started preparing 12 weeks in advance.

We knew we would never compete on any pro stage but it didn't stop us from wanting to look our best. We also knew that we would be close to the oldest people attending the show so we figured we'd give it our best shot, right? It was time for me to be the role model that I believe I'd been put on this earth to be. And, that's exactly what I did.

A former trainer of Stew's was participating in the Olympia. He was now married to one of the top fitness competitors, which gave us access and allowed us to be up close and personal with many of the other stars. We were thrilled. We also had accomplished our goal of being in top form and many of the younger competitors graciously complemented us, as did the people attending the Expo.

It was both exciting as well as an ego-boost. We were invited to our first after-party and really had no idea what to expect. Stew asked what time we should arrive and about died when he was told 11:30pm. Stew said he was never going to be able to stay awake. His old friend Craig suggested that we try this thing called "Ecstasy!" Neither one of us had ever heard of it let alone tried it but thought, what the hell, when in Rome.

I must confess it was really fun. It began a long journey of circuit parties and tons of fun, but the funniest thing is a photo that was taken of the two of us that night. I've never seen my eyes open so wide! I look like the cat that ate the canary! It was hilarious. We had a blast and looked forward to more pro shows and ended up going to the Arnold Classic, the massive fitness expo put on yearly by whom else but Arnold Schwarzenegger. There would be another after party and more fun to follow.

SEPTEMBER 1971

Back in September of 1971 after working all summer with mentally challenged kids on the south side of Buffalo, I met and dated Joe, my first Polish boyfriend (there's that Polish connection again). Months later, I found myself pregnant! Oops.

This was not a time when parents and children spoke about birth control, condoms, or safe sex. It was all taboo and knowing a bit more about my sexual past you can hopefully appreciate my predicament. I knew there was no way I could have a baby, let alone get any type of support from my parents so I knew I needed to figure this one out on my own.

I had returned from my high school graduation trip in California where I had spent 3 amazing weeks with my aunt and my cousin. All of my friends were back at school finishing up their senior year, but I had graduated and was now working full time as a nurse's aide at Children's Hospital in Buffalo.

I knew lots of doctors and nurses. I asked one of my female co-workers if she knew of a doctor who could help me and she gave me the name of Dr. Jack Lippes, the creator of the Lippes Loop. He just happened to have an office near the hospital. I called and made an emergency appointment.

I was only five weeks pregnant at best and was told that if Dr. Lippes inserted his Loop into my uterus while I was less than ten weeks pregnant it would cause a spontaneous abortion. It seemed to be my best choice. I knew that I did not want to experience the wrath of my parents, nor did I want to stop seeing Joe, which I knew they would insist upon.

So, after getting permission to leave early from my job, I took the bus to Dr. Lippes office to have the procedure. It involved opening my cervix. In other words they were forcing my uterus to go into LABOR! So, as much the procedure was going to help my situation, it really hurt in more ways than one!

And God, was it painful. I had to go back to work to wait for my mother to come fetch me. I had to act like I was fine! It was one of the most uncomfortable rides I have ever taken. I had to pretend I was in a bad mood because I knew if I looked into her eyes she would know that something was very wrong. I managed to get my best friend to take me to the movies where I sat in the dark, downing aspirin and Darvocet to deal with the pain! It was a very dark day in my life.

SEPTEMBER 29, 2015

My Mom died on September 29, 2015.

It's sad the way it happened. Mom had been living in a nursing home for nine months. I am unsure why, but so many things in my life seem to revolve around nine months patterns. Mom was content living there. Like me, she was a very friendly person to strangers and was enjoying the unit she'd been assigned to, one for people with dementia and Alzheimer's.

She had been diagnosed with Dementia. It was very difficult for me to see this once body and fashion conscious athletic woman put on 40 pounds of fat due to what she was being fed. Even more disturbing was to see her push a baby carriage around the unit. When we would ask her what she was doing, she'd say; "I'm pushing abound my baby, whose name is Guido", which of course had been my father's name!

She was as sweet as she could be, always smiling and looking happy. Please don't misread or misunderstand my comments to mean that my Mom wasn't this person in her earlier life, she was, but only to anyone outside of our house and family. She somehow put so much pressure on herself to be a perfect parent that it made her stiff and rigid at home. Sadly, I can see so much of her in me. I just pray that when the time is right I will be secure enough in myself to warrant one great relationship. It is one of my goals and my great hope.

In this scenario with my mom, I was looking at a sweet, little-old-lady, who did not resemble the mother that I knew. My siblings and I joked about her sweetness during this period saying maybe we just needed to feed her all along for her to be happy! I think the more meaningful aspect of this change in my mom is that once I saw it, I began to grieve for her three months before she passed, making her death a bit less intense if that's even possible.

I talked about the physical affect my mother's had on my blood pressure in the July chapter. What is important is what happened the day before she died and at the moment of her death. I must admit that up until the last couple of years I did not know that I was a drama queen, but I was. For years I just thought I was a victim. But, I now believe that I created these dramas to teach myself lessons and that I did create a pretty amazing life and all the stories that go with it.

The phone call came from my sister on September 25th telling me that mom, who had fallen out of bed head first, was dying! It happened to be the same day that Stew and I were saying goodbye to one another. We had just finished packing up the 17-foot truck with all the belongings that he would drive back to Texas. It was the final goodbye. We had already gotten divorced but were now solidifying it by breaking up what had been our home. It was amicable but still intense.

I was mentally exhausted and truly didn't feel compelled to jump on a plane to say good-bye to my mother in person because as far as I was concerned, the mom that I knew my whole life was already dead. Wow. That was a revelation to me, but that was the way it felt.

Perhaps if I was already settled into my condo and knew where my suitcases were, I would have gone back home in a heartbeat. But I was up to my knees in alligators and was physically and mentally exhausted. Lots of life events were ending for me. Thinking back to that day, it was as if my mom knew that her work on earth was done. I was finally ready to be myself for the first time in *my* life. I was capable of caring for myself, so she was free to go be with my dad.

I checked in with my family every day and a few days later, on September 28th; I went to Oscar's for the weekly T-dance. I needed to be with my close friends and get spiritually healed at my Church of Choice. I remember someone commented about how odd it was to see me dressed in black and jokingly asked if I was in mourning. Their face dropped when I said yes. But the date of September 28 was also significant because I believed that this day was the day that I had been conceived 60 years earlier!

In my mind it would have been poetic justice for her to pass away on that day and actually expected to get a phone call saying so, but instead was told that she was hanging on. I somehow managed to go to work on Monday the 29th but was mentally exhausted. I came home about 2pm and knew I needed to continue organizing my move and get my new place set up but I was too wiped out.

A friend was painting my living room and I was supposed to be helping him. I started to paint but then said that I needed to lie down. I went into my bedroom and lay on my back. I was having a strange stomachache and began rubbing my stomach. The ache was over my umbilical cord and I was rubbing and pressing on it thinking I had gas.

After a few minutes I noticed what felt like a knot in that area and started pressing on it harder when I felt something pop or break in me. It was a weird and scary sensation all at the same time. At the moment I felt it, I happened to lift my head up from the pillow to look down at the area and I saw the most unbelievable thing.

It looked like two hands came out of my stomach. They spread my belly button open and I saw dust blow out of the area. I know it sounds like an Alien movie sequel but I swear to you this is exactly what I saw.

Simultaneously, I made this huge gasp, loud enough that my friend in the other room asked it I was ok. I shared with him what happened and we were both silently dumbstruck! In my heart I knew this was my mom passing through me for the last time and imagined that the phone would ring any second confirming that she was gone.

Strangely the call didn't come. Instead, it came about two hours later. My oldest brother called to say that Mom had passed. With shaky voices, we both cried. I finally asked him what time she had died and he said that no one knew because she was in her room alone and was only discovered when they went back in to check on her.

But, I knew when her spirit left her body and came though mine.

We are connected to our mothers for nine months through our umbilical cord so it only made sense that I would feel something breaking in mine 60 years later. I am so very grateful for that unusual experience and keep it close to my heart. She always said that I was the child that was the most like her and even though it's considered bad taste for a mother to admit, told me that I was her favorite. I think it was true.

OCTOBER

OCTOBER 1964

In 1964 the band director came to my fourth grade class to ask if any of us were interested in playing an instrument. I was thrilled because I knew I wanted to play the drums. I don't know why. I didn't know any drummers but I just knew that was what I wanted to do. Now if you have ever seen me dance you know that my feet keep up with the beat of the drums. It's almost uncanny what my feet can do and I don't know where this talent came from but it is definitely apparent to all who know me. I do not come from a family of dancers nor musicians, but I seemed to have both talents inside of me and am ever so grateful for them.

We were given a permission slip to give to our parents granting us their good wishes to play. I dutifully brought mine home, told my parents that I wanted to play the drums, and they happily signed the form. Interestingly, they never challenged my choice of instruments. I was very happy and excitedly dropped off my slip the next day. A few hours later I was called out of class to go to the music room to meet with Mr. D.

He was a handsome man with smiling eyes and I instantly felt a connection to him as well as felt quite safe with his manner. We hit it off and as the saying now goes; "he had me at hello!" We chatted very briefly before he told me that he needed to talk to me about my choice of instruments. I wasn't quite sure what he meant but listened intently as he told me "girls were not allowed to play the drums!" I was beyond shocked but being the repressed and eager to please girl that I was, shyly murmured; "Ok, then what should I play? He suggested the clarinet to which I quickly agreed. As an aside, my parents never questioned the school's ridiculous rule forbidding girls to play the drums, so I became a clarinet player, appeasing everyone but myself. I've mentioned before that I was raised with the edict that children should be seen and not heard but there was also another rule to that adage that said that the adult was always right. Who was I to complain or contradict this adult? He told me where I had to go to rent my instrument and that was that. Quite quickly, I became very good at reading music and playing the clarinet. I sat first chair right way which made me the lead clarinetist in the band but even more than that, I became Mr. D's prodigy and the band's mascot which made me thrive. Mr. D. nicknamed me Jillsie, I don't know why, but I loved it. And everyone in the band called me that. I had never been the teacher's pet prior to this but I certainly was making up for lost time with Mr. D.

Whenever a decision was to be made by the band as a whole, Mr. D. would ask me what I thought we should do and for the life of me, and for reasons I have only begun to understand and appreciate now, I strongly stated my opinion! It was as if he knew that I needed to speak my mind; that I had something important to say and, perhaps he felt a little guilty for telling me I could not play the drums. All I know is that I felt heard, understood, and like I was a part of something; all feelings I had little to no experience with at home. I remained his pet until 10th grade when I discovered marijuana and eventually dropped out of band replacing it with sex, drugs, and rock and roll!

OCTOBER 22, 1999

October is the month that my Dad was born and in 1999 I flew to Rome to meet my parents to celebrate my Dad's birthday. They had flown ahead and were waiting for me at our relative's home in Udine, Italy, close to my grandmother's hometown.

It was my first time flying into the Rome airport where I rented a car to drive the six hours north to join them in Udine. It was the first time in my life that I almost walked off with someone else's suitcase and vice versa and, since it was no ordinary suitcase, it made it an even weirder situation and quite a weird welcome to Italy.

This was long before luggage made a fashion statement and in the days when most people's suitcases were black. I had purchased a large oversized, red-cloth suitcase so that I could spot it more easily. Well evidently "my twin" was travelling the same day and had the same idea. We were both walking out of the airport after waiting for 45 minutes to get our bags when this happened.

It was unseasonably hot on this particular October day and I was dressed in leather pants, which were now dripping wet. I was exhausted as well and just wanted to fetch my rental car and get on the road. As a result, I did not check the luggage tag when I saw what I assumed was my unique bag coming down the conveyer belt.

By chance, I noticed a person with an identical bag heading out the door. I bolted ahead and made a joke about us both having great taste. We both chuckled when I added; "By the way, that one is yours, isn't it?" We both stopped just long enough to glance at our tags, realizing that we had both grabbed the wrong bag! Welcome to Italy!

Once in my rental car, and since this was a year before I would get a cell phone, I took a map with me to chart the way. I'm not sure what I did wrong, but I suddenly had this weird feeling that I was heading west and not north and pulled over to the side of the road only to discover that sure enough I had taken a wrong turn. Sadly the next exit was 50km down the road and there was nowhere to do a U-turn! Welcome to Italy.

Angrily, I drove west for the 50km, beating myself up as I went. I must say I panicked again when I got to the tollbooth because I had neglected to go to the cambio to change any of my money into Lire. Thankfully, the teller was nice and gave me a free pass. I made it to Udine about 5 hours later having sped the entire way to make up time and met up with my parents, who were anxiously awaiting my arrival.

We spent the next week travelling down to my favorite city, Florence. We stayed in a pension near the city center close to the bicycle shop whose owner had the same name as my father's. We ate many meals at the Farmer's Market, which continues to be one of my favorite things to do in Florence, along with visiting museums, shops, and of course the churches and all the many, many, bridges.

For the life of me I can't remember how it came to be, but my father and I got into a fight the day of his birthday. It had something to do with which restaurant we were going to eat at for his birthday dinner. My dad was the epitome of frugal, a trait which I both respected but sometimes hated. By his choice, dad was picking up the bills for our trip, but each time that a bill was paid he would become uncomfortable and you could see the wheels turning in his head. We had eaten at very inexpensive meals up to this point when I suggested that we do something more special since he was turning 75! I'm not sure why but he really didn't want to spend the money and I might have insinuated that he was being cheap, something that had never before been spoken out loud.

Thankfully, we did make it to nicer restaurant for dinner but it was less than enjoyable and the air thick with unspoken tension. The good news is that the next day he did offer to take me shopping, something that had only occurred a few times in my life. He bought me a few nice items, which I still have and wear today. I think this might have been his way of apologizing. Funny the things that one remembers.

Although this was my third visit to Italy, I had never been through Tuscany. My sister had bought my Dad the book, "Under the Tuscan Sun" for his birthday and all three of us were taking turns reading it. We went to the same cities that the book described and had a wonderful time reminiscing about the scenes we liked from the book. The movie wouldn't be released till 2003.

 One day on our way to Assisi, an amazing thing happened to me. As we were driving through the gorgeous and rich landscape, its rolling hills covered in deep green grasses setting off the hues of the rich, red, earth I was moved in a way that was very new to me. I told my parents that I needed to pull off the road for a minute. They asked if I was okay to which I said, yes but that I just needed to get out of the car. I pulled over to the side of the road and got out of the car where they curiously followed me.

I got down on my knees and started digging in the dirt. I've never done anything like this before so I didn't know what to make of it except to imagine that perhaps I had lived here in another life and was having some type of flashback. I was so overcome with emotion and I wept as my hands touched the soil that had obviously touched my soul. A few minutes later, after I composed myself, we all got back into the car and continued the trip. My parents never mentioned a word to me about this and we carried on like nothing happened which I find rather interesting, don't you?

Off in the distance you could see Assisi, sitting majestically atop a hill where we were going to visit the graves of both St. Francis and St. Clare. Again, I became overwhelmed with emotion and cried the entire drive up to the top of the hill where the Basilica of St. Francis sits. The setting, the Basilica, and the remains of St. Clare who is interred there, moved me to tears. It's amazing to see the almost perfect skeleton of someone who was living 800 years ago!

Our last stop was to spend the night in Rome before flying home to our respective cities. We went around the corner from the pensione for drinks before dinner, finding a tiny osteria where we sat at the bar next to another couple. We began to chat with them and swapped travel stories. They were very nice and we were all enjoying ourselves when a few loud guys came into the bar and stood close behind our group. They had a quick drink and then they left. We didn't think much about it until we were ready to leave. We finished our drinks and said goodbye to the other couple. As we stood up to leave, the woman of the couple noticed that her purse was missing!

We were all mortified, realizing that it had happened right under our noses! The two men patted themselves down to thankfully find that they still had their wallets and mom and me, our purses. The owner called the Policia and we waited with the couple till they arrived and took our statements. They told us that this was a daily occurrence in Europe.

Welcome to Italy! All in all it was a very memorable trip!

OCTOBER 1997

October was also a great month for Matt and me to go on our separate buying trips to eastern Europe. The weather was still halfway decent and it was before the holidays and the ski season so the store was usually not too busy. This particular October I was going on my own and was both nervous and excited to be in charge of all the buying.

Matt had found a wonderful translator, Monika, who is still a dear friend today. She had a beautiful British accent and when I first met her I assumed she was from England. I had never seen the spelling of her name and imagined she was Monica from England rather than Monika from eastern Europe. So, you can imagine her surprise when I complimented her on her perfect accent. We still laugh about it today!

Monika would be accompanying me to the small towns where I would meet with the artists in their homes to buy the wooden sculptures and other handmade work that they so beautifully crafted. I knew a few key phrases and words to get by, but it sure helped to have her with me. That way, nothing would be, as they say, lost in translation.

We were on the final part of our journey and were spending a few days in the beautiful mountains of eastern Europe when a totally unforeseeable thing happened.

We were saying our goodbyes to our host, a lovely woman who paints on glass using the technique known as reverse painting (she paints on the reverse side of glass, essentially backwards!). The Citroen, which Matt had purchased for us a few years earlier, was packed and ready to go. I was parked at the top of her incredibly steep and icy driveway. I released the parking break before starting the car. I don't know why I did this but between the weight of the car and the ice on the driveway, the car started slipping backwards on its own, gaining momentum very quickly, so much so that I could not gain control of the car nor stop its motion!

Monika was screaming and I was trying not to freak out. The car crossed the thankfully empty road and began to slide backwards down the mountain on the other side of the street, which was a forest thick with trees. Now, why there was a patch of land with no trees at that exact spot is beyond me but I was grateful that we didn't immediately slam into a tree. However, I also did not know how I was going to be able to stop the out-of-control car. I had tried to use the emergency brake when we first began to slide, but it had snapped in two, rendering it useless. The forest was thick with Linden trees that are both very large and old and it took a one huge one to stop us dead in our tracks.

By this time our host had run down her driveway and was on her way to where we were stuck. I'm sure she was relieved to see that the car was still intact and in one piece. She ran down to see how *we* were inside the car. Outside of feeling extremely guilty and incredibly stupid, I was fine and Monika, who was now calm, came to realize that she, too, was fine.

We got out of the car and carefully made our way to the back of it to see what kind of damage had been done. Thankfully Citroens are very heavy cars weighing about 2500 pounds and since it was manufactured back in the 80's when they used steel for their bumpers, it was literally damage-free!

Now that we were all fine, we had to get the car out of the forest. Since there was no AAA in the town we had to rely on calling a local tow truck. A towing company came up to assess the situation only to tell us that the tow truck didn't have the power to pull a car that was halfway down the side of a mountain. Instead they suggested getting a large charter bus to tow us out which is what we did in the end.

The men who were assisting us were absolutely cracking up, laughing and shouting in their native language. Although I pretty much knew what the men were saying, I asked Monika to interpret. She told me that they were saying something like; "Who is this crazy American woman that was trying to drive backwards down the mountain?" and "Leave it to a woman!" I was mortified yet grateful to be alive and unhurt. It took about 2 hours to pull our unscathed car out of the forest. Now, with our egos intact and our stomach's full from the delicious food that our host made for us, we got back on the road and headed back to Monika's town many kilometers away. However, it appears that the Gods were still testing us, as we had to drive through a heavy snowstorm for the next six hours! Eventually, we arrived, safe and sound, and the whole trip was a great success. And believe it or not, that car is still running today!

OCTOBER 2007

October is also the month that Bodybuilding Stew and I had a number of wild rides. This time the ride was on a boat. We were sea-bound yet again and went on two more Atlantis cruises and both resulted in very odd experiences. I could not understand what was happening to me until I did a little more research. As I mentioned in the June chapter, I was born while Mercury was in Retrograde. As time went on, I began to learn more about its effects on people born during a retrograde cycle.

It is said that we are affected ten days prior to the retrograde cycle, which is normally 21 days, as well as ten days after! So, to sum it up; if the regular retrograde cycle is 21 days and you add an additional 20 days to it; then multiply it by the three or four times a year when it occurs, you're talking about 120 days of Mercury Retrograde energy per year! That's about three months a year or one quarter of the year, which I think sucks!

I didn't know it at the time but when I went back to check the dates of the cruises, sure enough, they both took place during a Retrograde cycle! This trip started out great. We left for the Mexican Riviera from Long Beach where we were drinking and partying our way south, enjoying the Military Party and the Opening Dance Party. We stayed up late and danced till the sun came up and then, BAM, three days into it, I was paralyzed. Not really paralyzed physically but instead totally numb to my surroundings. I didn't want to party and if I did, I was dull, (which if you know me is saying a whole bunch). I felt bored and basically unhappy as well.

I valiantly tried to fake it, pretending I was having a good time, but that only lasted a few hours. By the end of the trip I was depressed and bummed out. It took me a few weeks to shake it off. I finally let it go, chalking it up as a fluke but when the same thing happened a second time on the next cruise, I was totally bummed out. I mean who goes on a cruise to be depressed, isolated, and bored? Not me, that's for certain! This coming January of 2018 will be my first Atlantis cruise in almost ten years! And it is not during a Retrograde Cycle.... just saying!

Since then I have opted out on any fall cruises that occur before, during or after Mercury is in a retrograde phase. The way I view this is the day that I can go on one of these cruises during a retrograde phase will mean that I am really balanced and in charge of myself, so look out!

OCTOBER 7, 2013

I mentioned in the May chapter, that while on my Camino with Stew I ended up with plantar fasciitis and stopped half way through it to recover. We had taken the trip to see if we still had feelings for one another and although we didn't finish the trip together, we also didn't finish the relationship either. I believed that this heel pain seemed to reference my own difficulty in taking the next step towards divorce and moving forward with those plans; so in early October, Stew and I decided to give it one more try just to prove, or disprove, my theory.

Stew was going to come to Palm Springs to attend a fund-raiser that I had put together for a close friend and client of mine who owned a music school. I would be sharing my experience on the Camino, as it had gained such popularity in 2013 based on the movie; "The Way." Stew would be in the audience and would be able to share his experience as well.

The very next day we had planned to drive up to the Wine Country in Northern California to see if there was any hope of a reconciliation for us. The trip did not go well for me in many ways and I numbed myself just for us to be together. I knew this was the sign I was looking for and got up the nerve on the way home to ask him for a divorce.

It was one of the hardest things I have ever done. My voice was strong and I knew I would have to be the one who asked for the divorce.

Thank God Stew and I had such love and respect for one another that we were able to agree to the terms of a divorce over a cup of coffee at Starbucks, saving us humiliation, unnecessary pain, and a lot of money! Divorce is never easy but this made the process as painless as I think it could ever be and has allowed us to remain close friends and confidantes even today. Thank you, Stew, and you know I will always love you!

NOVEMBER

NOVEMBER 1981

Vince and I had been living together in Chicago for 16 months and things had really begun to deteriorate. His drinking had once again escalated and since he was working swing shifts it greatly affected any sense of normalcy or peace at home. There were many nights that he would come home drunk and force himself on me. I would just lie there face down and take it rather than make waves or attempt to say no or try to control him. I was working for the Visiting Nurse Association at the time and really loved my job. I thankfully had made a few close friends who had become my new support system. Babs, who is still one of my close friends today was one of my biggest advocates and the friend whom I relied on most when things were bad with Vince.

I had become disenchanted and disillusioned with my relationship and one day while doing my laundry at the local Laundromat met a guy who intrigued me. We flirted the way one does when you can't confront your unhappiness and instead begin to act out emotionally and eventually sexually. I ended up accepting a dinner invitation from him on a night that Vince would be a work. I knew his habit was to go out after work with the guys for drinks and that he would come home drunk long after midnight. I knew in my heart that it was wrong for me to go but did it anyway. I again felt powerless.

The guy and I had a decent enough time, did some superficial kissing and petting before I left to go home. What I didn't know is that Vince had left work early that day and arrived home long before I got there. He had been drinking heavily and was both drunk and high. I was mortified and scared to death when I realized the score. As soon as I opened the door of our third floor apartment, I knew I was in serious trouble.

He verbally attached me and since I had been out with another man I felt very guilty and bad. He didn't mince his words and made it perfectly clear that I was in big trouble. He forced me to sit on the couch and would not let me get up. I was very frightened of him and felt totally helpless. He began to verbally abuse me and was yelling at me so loudly that our landlady had to come upstairs to tell him to keep it down. She was an elderly eastern European woman who had been very motherly to us both and as much as I wanted to tell her that I was in danger, I didn't want to involve her or get her in the middle of what I knew was going to be an ugly situation. She finally went back downstairs after a few minutes and as soon as she closed the door he threatened to really hurt me if I made a sound. I was his prisoner and was being held captive.

I sat on the couch for the next 2 hours while Vince paced back and forth shooting me hateful looks and saying horrific things to me in hushed tones. Around 11:30pm his two best friends came over to see what was going on. I was grateful to see them. As soon as I could, I secretly motioned to them that I was afraid of what he was going to do to me. They could tell he was out of control and tried to calm him down. One of them got him into the kitchen while I told the other that he had basically imprisoned me on the couch and that I was in fear of my life.

We made a plan that as soon as he passed out, which would most likely happen soon, they would come back to the apartment to get me. I felt relieved to know that we had a plan and prayed that it would work. Finally around 2am he passed out. I called the

2 boys and asked them to bring their truck. I was not leaving, I was moving out!

Over the next 3 hours while Vince was in a drunken stupor we moved me out hook line and sinker. I had furnished most of our apartment and felt compelled to take every single thing that belonged to me. I'm not sure how we did it but around dawn we were done. Vince was now alone in his bed with the things he owned prior to my moving in with him. I was now being driven to the suburbs where his best friends lived to unpack my belongings and try to gather my senses. I had to be at work in a few hours and was, of course, in shock.

At about 6:30am the phone rang and it was Vince. He had just woken up to find out that not only was I was gone but that I had completely moved out too! He was beyond freaked out and was in shock as you could only imagine. He didn't know where I was or where I had gone or how I had managed to move everything out. His friends of course couldn't tell him what they had just done and had to commiserate with him. It was a total trip. By this time, I was totally exhausted and had decided to call in sick to work. I called Babs who was going to cover for me till I could get my act together.

I finally fell into a deep sleep. A few hours later, I was woken up by the guys who told me that Vince was on his way over to their house. I had to go into the garage and hide until he was gone. It was one of the most surreal moments of my life. I could hear him ranting and raving and taking no responsibility for his part in the whole thing. His friends allowed him to vent but never let on as to how they really felt about the situation and he eventually left. The three of us were exhausted by this point and finally collapsed.

I got ahold of the Chicago newspaper and began perusing the want ads to find myself an apartment, which I did. By that weekend, again with the help of his friends, I moved into my first solo apartment up in Roger's Park just south of Evanston, Illinois. I eventually called Vince to tell him where I was but to this day he never knew how I moved out or who helped me! Believe it or not we toyed with dating again, went out a few dozen times during the holiday season but by early January finally ended our relationship for good. It's amazing for me today to see all these same patterns but had no idea of them at the time. Life is really interesting when you are paying attention.

November is my month of beginnings where January was my month of endings. Being that Thanksgiving marks the beginning of the holiday season, a time for many of us to feel alone, lonely, unloved, unwanted, or not good enough can result in depression, something that I know about personally. So as it goes, I unconsciously started many new relationships the Wednesday before Thanksgiving Day that all strangely ended the first couple of weeks in January, or the end of the holiday season. Here's pretty much the way it went down.

I've mentioned that I was born and raised in Buffalo, N.Y., a city that once had the honor of being known for having more bars per capita than any other city in the country! Hey, now that's novel, right? Well, what this meant for us Buffalonians is that we were always at bars! Legally or illegally, that is what we went for our entertainment, and I was most likely the leader of the pack!

I mentioned that my Grandmother owned a tavern so maybe bars were in my blood. Every year on the

Wednesday before Thanksgiving day, I went to the bars and inevitably met someone while dancing. I think I mentioned that I was not a dater, but instead had relationships so, whomever I met that pre-holiday night would most likely become "my new boyfriend!"

I could play all the holiday games that people play. I could buy gifts and feel like I had a boyfriend; or I could go to a New Years Eve party with a date rather than go alone and of course had someone to go church with on Christmas Eve night or mass the next day.

It also helped diffuse the tension in my family home by having an outsider present, which shifted the focus off of me. During all of those teen/early adult years, both my sister and brother were married and had a built in buffer of a spouse; whereas my youngest bro and I had none, making us more of a target for criticism something that always seemed to creep its way into our get togethers! So, by having my own holiday date made things a bit more tolerable for me. I was totally unaware of my behaviors back then, but I'm sure aware now!

NOVEMBER 1974

Back in November of 1974, while in Nursing School, I was working part-time in a Sporting Goods Store in Buffalo. This is where I met Vince. It was love at first sight! We'd been flirting at work for a few weeks until he finally asked me out. I was ecstatic and could barely contain myself. Is this beginning to sound familiar?

I have had the same fantasy since my first flirtation with the opposite sex. This person was going to be the "one". They were going to rescue me and all my problems would be solved. We would fall in love and get married. And that was a far as it ever got! There was no fantasy about a wedding, a house, home or kids. Just falling in love, plain and simple.

Our first date was on a Friday night. Since he did not have a car, I was going to pick him up and drive us to the movies. As it happened, my car was in the shop after a bad oil repair job, so I asked my oldest brother if I could borrow his Dodge Dart, to which he agreed.

We excitedly held hands the whole way through the movie, necking along the way. I was not a virgin at this point and knew from the way he kissed me that I wanted to go all the way with him. Yes, that's how easy I was!

Little did we know but, while we were in the theater, Buffalo was being dumped on yet again. Because of its close proximity to Lake Erie, Buffalo had some of the worst snowstorms in the country and this one ended up being one of the worst snowstorms in its history. But, Vince and I were totally in the dark, if you get my drift! (Couldn't resist!)

The movie let out around 11:00pm and we were amazed to see what had happened while we were getting to know each other better. We also realized that we were most likely going to be stranded because there was now close to three feet of snow on the ground.

However, that was not going to stop me from trying to at least get us to Vince's parents house where he lived. It was closer to the theater than my dormitory. We made it to the entrance of his street where we abandoned the car and walked the remaining ¼ mile to his home.

As soon as we got inside, I called my brother to let him know what happened and then got introduced to Vince's parents, who had obviously been drinking. I'm not trying to be critical or judgmental but it was pretty apparent. Drunk or not, they graciously invited me to spend the night. Vince and I both drank and smoked pot and his parents seemed not to care that we were going down to the basement to do both. It was legal in N.Y. State at that time to drink at 18, so it really wasn't a big deal, but was not something that I typically did in front of my parents, so it made it more daring and exciting.

Vince had a pool table down there and a pretty decent music system so it was kind of like being in a private club. He had three older brothers, one of whom who lived in the basement as well, but in separate quarters. All three of the brothers liked to party and did so with one another. This was also new to me as my family lived quite separate lives. Eventually we got tired and it was time to go to bed.

Vince and I got high and of course the sexual tension rose; I mean this was a first date and I was now going to be spending the night with this guy, but in his family house. It had all the ingredients of danger and excitement. And even crazier was the fact that his Mom, well in this case, step-mom and his dad continued to drink upstairs and by 1:00am were in the bag!

Vince and I snuck up the backstairs to his bedroom when I started hearing what I thought was yelling and Vince's response to this was to turn the music louder while offering the explanation that this was a normal Friday night at his house. This was the first time in my life outside of a TV movie that I had ever heard two people yelling at one another. I remember the thrill I felt when I realized what was going on.

To be honest with you, my parents did not fight but there was so much tension in my house that I think I wished that they would yell at one another and get it over with. I was truly mesmerized and actually wanted to go downstairs to listen to it more closely, but didn't share this with Vince. Instead we went to bed and had great sex that night!

Well, I got snowed in and ended up staying at his house for 4 nights in a row! It was crazy! It was like an arranged marriage but at least was one where both partners were actually attracted to each other and very, very, sexually compatible!

And boy did we ever have a lot of great sex from that first night, right there in his bedroom, two doors down the hall from his parents, who would conveniently pass out after their fights! It was super cool in my mind. I was totally in love and so was he! Well, I'm sure we all know by now that it was a combination of youth and lust, but I was ecstatic! Yeah me!

By the third night, I knew the drill and but yet didn't realize that his parents had raised an alcoholic son, so when all three of them; the parents and Vince drank; I knew that it would end up in another fight.

Vince and I would go up to his room and have sex while the parents would stay downstairs and continue to drink. Vince would eventually pass out around the time that his parents would start to fight. I would sneak out of his bed, and sneak out of the bedroom and make my way to the top of the stairs where I would listen to their fights. I really got high off of this energy and it's only now that I can begin to understand it all.

NOVEMBER 1975

We continued to date for the next few years and the next November is when the so-called shit hit the fan or in this case, my nose.

We had a regular habit of staying at my parent's house while they were at the ski resort where I had my car accident all those years earlier, or we'd stay at Vince's parents house. This particular night was the Friday after Thanksgiving and I was off of school for a week. I normally would have been skiing with my parents, but wanted to stay in Buffalo to see Vince, so I lied and told them I would be working some shifts at the hospital. This meant that my parent's house would be empty and Vince and I could go there for more privacy.

We had been out at the bars, drinking and partying, and it was clear to me by now that Vince was an alcoholic, but I loved him and like so many other co-dependents, enabled his drinking while at the same time thinking I could save him! LOL!

We left the bar and as usual I was driving us back to the burbs. His behavior was escalating and he was becoming more obnoxious and unruly so I had decided that rather than take him to my parent's house for drunk-sex/sexual abuse that I would take him to his parent's house.

It was about 4am when we left the bar, which meant that the highway was relatively empty because if it had not been, I'm pretty certain I'd be dead. Here's what happened.

I passed the exit that was to take us to the burbs and Vince who, I thought had passed out, said, slurring his words, "You missed the exit!"

I replied; "No, I didn't, I'm taking you home!"

He did not like this one bit and screamed, "Get off the fucking highway, NOW!" and grabbed the wheel of my car, yanking it to the right, forcing me to cross four lanes of traffic before I could gain control of the car.

I was in shock and screaming, "Get your fucking hands off the steering wheel!" when his left fist struck me with full force in the middle of my nose, breaking it instantly, blood was running down my face and all over my clothes.

I don't know how I managed to get the car up the ramp and onto the street without crashing or losing control, but I did. I pulled down the first street I came to and stopped the car, slamming on the brakes.

I screamed, "GET THE FUCK OUT OF MY CAR!" and I think only because he was in shock that he get out.

As I sat there trying to catch my breath and stop the bleeding from my nose, his fist hit my driver's side window.

"OPEN YOUR FUCKING DOOR!" he screamed, trying to open my door and get into the car.

"I'll break your fucking window." he yelled. And the only reason I opened the door was because I figured that if he had already broken my nose he wouldn't stop at a window!

As soon as I opened the car door he grabbed me by my jacket and pulled me out of the car and threw me down onto the side- walk. He jumped on top of me and he proceeded to hit me in the face.

We did not know that the person whose house we were in front of us was an early riser, had heard the ruckus and called the police. They were happily only a few blocks away and were there almost immediately.

They saw him pummeling my face and jumped out of the patrol car, grabbing him from atop me, saying, "She's just a helpless little girl, who's half your size!"

I'm certain I was in shock, having lost blood and surviving this crazy situation but not enough so that I could make the right decision when the cops asked me if I wanted to press charges. I remember saying, "No, I don't want to press charges, I just want you to take him home and get him away from me!

When they told me that they could not take him home, but only to jail, I co-dependently knew what I had to do. I knew that we were both going to be in big trouble with our parents if I had him arrested and that was the only thing I could focus on, which I think is pretty interesting! I project into the future and avoid taking care of myself in the present.

So, I said, "No, I do not want to press charges." And then believe it or not, proceeded to drive him home!

Yeah, I know, it's pretty unbelievable to me too!

I really did not know how to take care of myself at all. I did not know how to set boundaries, how to say no or put myself first. I really had a long way to go and pray that I have finally arrived there now!

By the time I drove him home he had sobered up the way one does with all that adrenaline pumping. He also was incredibly remorseful, like all abusers.

But, I was not having it. This was the straw that broke the camels back. I was done with him!

I pulled up to his parent's driveway and ordered him to get out of my car. He pleaded with me to please come in so that we could talk but I said no, and again asked him to leave. The sun was just coming up and I was exhausted.

I realized that I needed to use the bathroom and agreed to come in and do so but then was going to immediately leave. When I saw my face in his parent's powder room mirror I was mortified. My nose was flattened on my face, which was already swelling up.

I just wanted to be alone and back in my dorm room. I used to do this really weird thing when I was beyond angry, which I was now. I would neither look at the other person nor talk to them and did this with Vince for 30 minutes while he tried to apologize.

I somehow had calmed down enough to I find the strength to drive myself to the dormitory. I also had enough wherewithal to stop at a 7-11 where I bought a ten-pound bag of ice. I put the ice on top of my face and slept for five solid hours in my room. Amazingly, when I woke up, all the swelling was down. I crossed the street and stepped into the E.R. where I was given cocaine nasal spray to fix my broken nose!

By the next evening, when the girls returned to the dorm from their family holiday weekend, I greeted them with my broken nose and 2 black eyes. They of course wanted to know what had happened, so I concocted the following story. I told them that I had been at our favorite Dance Club called Mickey Rats. I said that as I was coming back from the bathroom, I was hit face first by a waiter who was coming around the corner carrying a tray full of glasses! HAHAHA!

Whether they believed it or not, we all laughed and said how awful/funny/ironic it was and went on our merry way! Interestingly, it would be in November of 2001, almost 30 years later right before Thanksgiving day that I would have plastic surgery on my nose. I guess the nose knows!

On a final note, many of my closest friends and many family members are born in November, and a few on the same day and the same year! There is a lot of synchronicity in my life! Just saying......

DECEMBER

DECEMBER 1982

Babs, my best friend from the Visiting Nurse Association, introduced me to one of her friends named Joe. I know, another "J" name! Joe however was the first Hispanic man I had ever dated. He and I were instantly attracted to one another, had one date, and were immediately in a relationship. (Can you say "Pattern"?)

Joe was a nice guy but he was really depressed. I'm sure that in some way I believed that I could "fix" him but I, too, was very depressed back in those days. I think that some of the choices I made in boyfriends were people who were sicker than I was which, in turn, made me feel better about myself.

Joe was the first boyfriend that had a motorcycle and we took a few day trips together and had a great time. We were together for a few months and things were going okay but I sensed that he was very insecure and very jealous. His depression was quite intense and no matter how much I tried to listen to him and help him believe in himself, it was not working. He was on anti-depressants and saw a therapist on a regular basis but he just couldn't seem to get any better. I knew that the relationship was not going to be long term.

A few weeks later, my old boyfriend, Polish Joe, called me out of the blue. I was so happy to hear from him and since we hadn't talked in many years we spent a long time on the phone catching up. He had always wanted to spend time in Chicago and since I was now a grown up girl, living and working in the big city, I excitedly invited him to come stay with me. This had been a dream of mine for years and I was beyond ecstatic. I had so many fantasies about what was going to happen and couldn't wait for his visit.

I had already pulled back from my Hispanic, Local Joe, who wasn't dealing with it very well. We were not really dating at this point but still communicating on a regular basis. I had to break the news to him that Polish Joe was going to be visiting me and made it perfectly clear that we had some unfinished business and that I needed my space. He was understandably very upset but realized that he couldn't change the situation or control me.

Polish Joe came to visit and we had the most unbelievable time. There was an intimacy during those first days that we had never had before and I was convinced that we were going to get back together. I had wanted to marry him ten years earlier and actually thought we were going to have the opportunity to do so this time around. Unannounced and uninvited, Local Joe came to meet the "other" Joe and it was incredibly awkward.

Polish Joe and I continued to have fun, going to the dog track and out for meals and movies. It was all going really well. The intimacy was incredible and in the way I knew it could always be. I was sure we were going to re-unite and that this time it would be for good. A few days later, I came home from work to find his suitcases by the door. I was shocked! I thought maybe someone in his family had died and I questioned him as to what was going on. He told me that he was freaked out by the intimacy and needed to leave. For the first time in *my* life, I realized that I actually had power over another person as opposed to that person having power over me.

I wasn't being rejected by a man.

Instead, he was showing me that he couldn't deal with his own feelings. It was a big moment in my life. I very sadly took him to the airport where we said a long goodbye. I knew in that moment that we would never pass this way together again.

However, a few weeks later in January, something beyond my wildest imagination would transpire that would truly change my life forever. I received a phone call from Babs asking if I had seen or heard from Local Joe, to which I said no, I had not. I asked why and she said that none of his friends had heard from him in awhile and people were beginning to get concerned that something bad had happened. I instantly knew that this situation was not going to end well.

Hours later I got the dreaded phone call telling me the worst possible news. Joe had committed suicide. He had shot himself. He was found by one of his friends, who had gotten the police to break into his house. I was heartbroken and in shock. Part of me felt guilty and perhaps somewhat responsible. I mean I was the last person who had broken up with him and maybe that's what finally pushed him over the edge.

I had many thoughts about the situation after I hung up the phone. I remained very sad and depressed and then somewhere out of the blue I found myself thinking about Joe's mother. I was the only friend who had ever met her.

Joe had wanted us to meet for many reasons but specifically because we were both nurses. She was a very closed-down person and did not seem at all happy to meet me. Joe's dad had been dead for years and Joe and his mother had a very difficult relationship, at best.

I called Babs to ask if anyone had talked to Joe's mother and she said no. I knew she didn't like me very much but I knew she needed to know about her son. I did not have her phone number or know where she lived but I did know where she worked. I ended up calling her at the hospital knowing that it was a very poor choice on my part but I felt helpless and conflicted. I asked to speak to Joe's mother's supervisor. I explained who I was and why I was calling. I asked her opinion about how to handle the situation and then asked if she would take responsibility to support her after I broke the news. She agreed to assist.

Joe's mother came to the phone and I had to tell her that there had been an accident and that Joe was dead. As you can imagine there was a very long silence before she asked what happened. I did my best to tell her what had been told to me all the while telling her how very sorry I was. A few minutes later she ended the call.

It was one of the most difficult things I have ever had to do and hope that I will never have to be in that role again. We buried Joe the following week. I was glad to see the small church so full of people who loved him. Joe's mom was, of course, distraught but managed to allow me to stay close to her during the service, which made me feel useful in some small way. I was so sorry that she hadn't been able to show that side of herself while Joe was alive. I will never forget him and hope that if we are ever reincarnated, in his next life he will be much better than the one he left so abruptly.

CHRISTMAS 1985

I was living in Chicago in 1985. My best gay friend, Todd (who was now also now my boyfriend) and I had rented a car and were planning to leave Christmas Eve morning to drive eight hours to Buffalo, N.Y. to spend the holiday with my family. We planned on leaving about 5am and were to arrive in Buffalo in time for Christmas Eve dinner at my bother and sister-in-law's house. My best girlfriend, Laurie, was set to fly into Buffalo from Atlanta, GA. and would land around 4:00pm Todd and I had planned to pick her up at the Buffalo International Airport.

As luck would have it, the forecast reported that a huge snowstorm was supposed to be hitting Chicago early on December 24th making us a bit nervous to get on the road as soon as possible. We managed to get the rental car started and Todd said he would drive. I had grown up in snow and had driven in it for many years but since Todd was the man and said he wanted to drive, I agreed, thinking to myself that he must be capable.

It began to snow as we left downtown Chicago. At first it was a mild, lake effect, snowstorm but by the time we hit the interstate it was really snowing hard. Thankfully there was little to no wind. We were about 25 minutes into the drive, and dawn was maybe 15 minutes away when the winds picked up on the interstate and the visibility dropped to about 15 feet! Up ahead we saw a large green "item" in the road. It appeared to be a large green garbage bag but instead turned out to be one of the large green signs one sees on the highway that says, "Next exit 1 mile", or something to that effect! It was only when we were right on top of it that we realized what it was and Todd swerved to avoid hitting it. We did hit the sign but thankfully did not lose control of the car!

We immediately pulled over to see what damage had been done. Miraculously, the sign punctured the rear wheel well but did not damage the tire! Todd was beside himself and I knew he could not continue to drive. I told him that I was perfectly capable of driving and would take over, which I did.

At this point we were in a white out! The visibility was zero and outside of a few large trucks on the highway we were alone. We saw many cars that had veered off the road and were stuck or snowed in. But the driving Gods were with me and I managed to carefully follow the taillights of the semis and drove no faster than 20 mph for the next six hours.

It was now 11am and we were only one third of the way to Buffalo. The weather never cleared but we finally made it to Buffalo at 8pm that night. My parents had picked up Laurie and gotten acquainted with her while waiting for us to arrive. To this day, Todd thinks I am a Rock Star and believes I can do just about anything! But even with that luck, the trip was not a good one for me. Like so many people, I reverted back to the old childhood feelings I had of being insecure, depressed, and angry. It certainly helped to have my friends there but I still allowed myself to get triggered by my family.

DECEMBER 1, 2000

Jumping decades, Stew and I had planned to get married on December 2, 2000, the first Saturday in December, typically the most popular day of the week to be wed. We were to be married in Houston, where he was from, rather than Santa Fe, N.M. where we lived because all of his family lived in Houston. It was also close enough to New Mexico that our friends could attend. And my family, who all lived on the East coast, had planned to attend and was treating it like a true vacation.

I started thinking about the timing of the wedding and my experiences with out of town weddings. I realized that it's typical for the bride and groom to fly off early Sunday morning to go to on their honeymoon. I knew that it might be difficult to relax with the people who had come so far to see us, so I decided that a Friday night wedding might be a better plan.

This way our families could fly in Thursday night, get situated at the Houstonian Hotel, where we would all be staying, and where we'd be getting married. This would allow us to have quality time together before the festivities started Friday night. Stew didn't care one way or the other, so I changed the wedding date to Friday, December 1, 2000.

Our December 1st wedding was to take place around 6:00pm following a one-hour cocktail party. Stew and I greeted and mingled with our guests. Everything was going great until I realized that Stew's Best Man, his oldest son from his first marriage, was not there. I asked Stew where he was and he said he didn't know but would try to reach him. I was anxious as it was and this delay was not what I had hoped for or wanted on my wedding day.

True, it was a second wedding, but this wedding was the real deal to me as my family, who'd not been present at my first wedding, was there. By 6:15pm I was really upset and told Stew that our guests were waiting and that we needed to get on with our ceremony. He said he wanted to wait for his son. Now, this is where it gets dicey for me. Stew had invited his deceased wife's family to the wedding as he was naturally still close to them. This included her mother and father, her sisters and his stepchildren along with his kids from his first marriage. It all made sense to me at the time that he suggested it but I found myself struggling with "our" decision on "my" day!

I'd like to believe that I am strong enough to handle everything that life throws at me, but for some reason this day was an exception. I had a lot of growing up to do, but as this was my wedding day, I was overly sensitive and was starting to feel lost at my own wedding. I wanted to shine and be the center of attention; this was my understanding of weddings and long before Bridezilla's were a thing. It was not happening!

Stew must have been under a lot of pressure as well. His deceased wife had only been gone for 15 months and her family was now watching him wed someone else. It must have been very bittersweet. I think you know by now that I am a very sensitive person and was most likely feeling everyone's sorrow and sadness as well as the joy of the day. I started having this sinking, lonely, feeling made worse by the fact that Stew could not reach his son by phone and did not know where he was. At some point it all got to me and like Julia Roberts (there she is again) in Runaway Bride, I bolted!

I left the cocktail hour and hid in our room. It would take my father and my sister to coerce me to rejoin the party and get married. His son finally showed up, drunk and high but he was actually there! Stew's dad, a Methodist minister, was to marry us. I'm delighted to report that I managed to re-balance myself enough to be able to walk down the aisle with love in my heart for Stew. The rest of the wedding went off without a hitch.

It is the actual date of December 1st that plays such an important role for me. Although I had a number of very close gay friends at that time, I was unaware that December 1st was International AIDS Day. This is very significant for me because today I am totally immersed in the gay community and it is one of the reasons that Stew and I eventually divorced. Today, I am the only female trainer at World Gym, the largest gay gym in Palm Springs and am known to many of my clients and most of my community as The Dancing Queen of Palm Springs.

How did it come to be that I would live and love amongst the gay community? Was I drawn there? I'd say absolutely. Am I meant to be there? Again, absolutely. Is it a chore, bother, or burden? Absolutely Not! Am I happy? Yes, I am! I am where I am supposed to be and maybe with a bit more history it will make more sense to you as well as it does to me.

When I was a child, I thought a lot about nuns, or more accurately, monks. I was a bit of an odd kid who did extra credit homework rather than play outside with my friends. While studying, I used to test myself to see how much stamina and control I had by holding my urine to see how long I could wait before having to pee! I was into denial and self-flagellation. My picking and my hair pulling and my always trying to help people all seemed to be traits that fit both nuns and monks.

Then there was my wish to be a surgeon, then a social worker, and finally a nurse, again, showing how driven I was to help others. I mentioned that I didn't have a good experience with nuns but the picture that I had in my mind, along with a little help from Sister Bertrille (The Flying Nun) made me wonder if this was my life's path.

I didn't know that most young girls fantasize about their wedding day. I guess they buy wedding magazines and pick out their wedding gowns and imagine what it would be like to walk down the aisle. I didn't know that they spent months thinking about their wedding receptions, cakes, songs, houses, honeymoons, and all the rest of it, because I was not that young girl. I wasn't close to my sister so we didn't play house or talk about such things. And my mother never encouraged me to talk about my future as a wife and mother, either. I did think that I would get married and have kids but that was about as far as my fantasizing went. So who knows, maybe I was supposed to be a nun but this didn't ever sync with my love of sex and men.

But, I did think a lot about deprivation and denial, so maybe I was channeling my past life as a monk! I'm sure most of it had to do with control and the lack of that component that I felt in my own life so the only way I could gain control was to decide when I would pee, or when I would eat or deprive myself. Anorexia and bulimia were also totally fitting for me, I just didn't understand any of it at the time, nor did anyone else. I was driven to control my body and exercised with vigor, doing 500 sit-ups a day by the time I was 12 and would do as many push-ups as I could, which is why my pecs are really over-developed.

I was pretty much a tomboy who loved to ride bikes and play softball. I kept trying to prove myself to the men in my family after subconsciously realizing that men ruled in my family home and that in it, women were second-class citizens.

If you can't beat 'em, join 'em!

When I think back to the type of men men I attracted when I was younger, I'm going to bet that at least half of them are gay today. Seriously, I went out with some really drop dead gorgeous men who were all shy, talented, uber-intelligent, and usually on the edge rather than in the center of the groups they related to. Many were loners.

I seemed to have this knack for making people feel comfortable and many of these guys would tell me that I made them feel understood for the first time in their lives. The sex between us was over the top and one guy, who'd been previously married, told me that what we shared after our first time was more intimate than he'd felt with his former wife of ten years!

I can see people's pain and intuit something that seems to get transmitted through my eyes. I have become the person that people confess things to and I tend to gain their confidence quite quickly. It's so beautifully perfect for me to be amongst the gay community. I feel a sense of fulfillment that is totally unique. I love these men like no others and am perfectly satisfied to live and work amongst them day in and day out.

This was very difficult for Stew to fully accept and I can certainly understand his feelings. I come alive around gay men. If you've ever been with me on the dance floor you will see what I am talking about. Quite often, gay men and I will comment about this connection and chalk it up to an energy that was established at the beginning of time. Other times, we've joked that I must have been a gay man in a past life and a very popular one at that! Regardless of the why's or how's, it was too much for Stew to handle and be comfortable with and it did change our relationship.

Once we found out that December 1st was International AIDS day, we would joke that I married him and the gay community on the same day. There is more than a grain of truth in that statement.

I take responsibility for my part in all of that, but I also know that the energy that courses through my veins when I am with gay men, has a life of its own and I chose to accept it rather than ignore it. Remember, I did have that epiphany at the White Party telling me to move to Palm Springs so there must be something much bigger than me at stake. Perhaps, like a good nun or monk, I heard "my calling" and obeyed.

So, when Stew and I came to realize and accept that our 12 year relationship had sadly run its course, it was no surprise to him or me that I would remain in Palm Springs when we mutually and respectfully divorced one another on December 31, 2013.

DECEMBER 14, 2008

On December 5th, my sister's birthday, I received a call from my mom.

She has called me JI for as long as I can remember and it was no different that day.

"JI, your dad is really ill. He was admitted to the ER and is now in intensive care", she said.

We had agreed that she would call me to come home when the end was in sight, so I said; "Is it time?" To which she quietly replied; "It is."

Back in 2005-6, Dad had been struggling with numbness on the left side of his face that was driving him crazy. He'd seen numerous doctors who could not determine the cause of or find the cure for his problem but most agreed that he was experiencing Trigeminal Neuralgia, a problem with one of the cranial nerves. He saw specialist after specialist until he met with a doctor who said she had seen a case like this once before and suggested doing a biopsy behind his eye. They found that he had a rare type of cancer and needed an operation to determine its severity.

Simultaneously, he was given an appointment at the Cancer Center Treatment of America, who suggested a much more palliative treatment involving radiation, nutrition and other less dangerous solutions. The difference between these two approaches was that Medicare would cover his surgery but not cover the Cancer Center approach. This meant that he would have to pay for the Cancer Center out of pocket. I'd mentioned that my dad was frugal and although I can't prove it, I fear his decision was 100% financial.

He agreed to have the surgery and was warned that it was very risky and could result in permanent damage if one of his cranial nerves was accidently clipped during the procedure. Sadly this is exactly what happened. My dad ended up with total paralysis on the left side of his face. He could not speak, smell, taste or swallow! Just imagine that, if you will. To my dad's credit I feel he made the right choice because his final diagnosis after surgery proved that he would have succumbed to death soon anyway

Now I am as vain as the next person, but I did not appreciate that my dad was as vain as he turned out to be. He refused to leave the house except to go to the doctors or occasionally to church. He did not want visitors and refused outside help. He was absolutely miserable. He was angry most of the time and no one knew how to help him. He refused in home nursing care, leaving all of his care to my mom. She has always been a go-getter and this time was no different, she did what she had to do.

My dad loved to eat and understandably was angry that he could no longer enjoy eating. He had a feeding tube and was living on protein shakes most of the time. My mom felt guilty about eating in front of him so she stayed in the corner of the kitchen, with her back to him and ate yogurt and cereal during the two years that he was dying. It was horrible. She weighed close to 110lb when he got ill and was now a bag of bones at 92 pounds!

It was only after his death that we were told that he died of Shingles of the Brain!

Dad had been born with Herpes Simplex 2 and suffered with cold sores most of his life. On a driving trip to Florida to visit my youngest brother and the grandkids, Dad had had an outbreak while driving the car and must have accidently picked at the cold sore and then unconsciously touched his eye, infecting himself. This happens in a tiny percentage of people and is not usually fatal, but none of us, including his doctors realized what had transpired so he was lead down this crazy path of eye surgery, paralysis and self-destruction and ultimately his death.

Dad had agreed to be a DNR, or a "Do Not Resuscitate", and was amazingly organized and focused to get his affairs in order for my mom. He was determined to ease her into being alone after 62 years of marriage and even bought her a new car so that she would be safe. Mom managed well, but doing all his caretaking alone took a toll on her and even though she managed to live on her own for six years following his death, she was never the same.

I doubt that I will ever have the opportunity to deal with a caretaking situation like this unless I miraculously get married tomorrow and live to be 144. But, for all you caretakers out there, please know that you must take care of yourself first in order to do more than survive your loved ones illness. It is critical for you and the health of your Body, Mind, and Spirit!

So, that December night when dad had fallen out of bed, my mom was forced to call the paramedics to assist him as she was too weak to pick him up on her own. The paramedics saw how ill he was, covered in blood both from where he had hit his head and where he'd been picking his scalp so they admitted him to the ER. There, he was treated with IVs, oxygen, and blood, which gave him and us, false hope that he was better. As a DNR, he should not have received any of this treatment but it happened anyway. This is when I came onto the scene.

By the time I flew into Buffalo, a full day trip from the West Coast, he was stable and out of ICU. We were informed by the staff that they could no longer keep him in the hospital because there was nothing else they could do for him and needed to discharge him to a nursing home or to our family home to die!

That was the gist of it and I was to be the person who was to ask him what he wanted to do. You can imagine the anxiety I felt!

"Dad, I have to talk to you about something really difficult and I need you to hear me." I said, as I held his hand. He couldn't talk but I saw his eyes open widely.

"The hospital can not longer keep you here and we have to make a decision as to where you will go from here."

I continued, " There are two choices. One is to go home, where we can all be with you till the end, or the other is to go to a nursing home."

"Do you understand?" I asked.

He nodded his head yes.

"Dad, mom is no longer able to take care of you, it's affecting her health and well being, she is frail and can no longer pick you up or take care of herself."

"I know this is a very difficult decision for you, but I want you to think about what it would be like if the roles were reversed."

At this point, his eyes had glazed over. I knew he was struggling with making the best decision but also knew that my mother was on overload. She had told me earlier that she didn't want him to come home and I know that I was trying to help her by getting him to go to the nursing home.

"Dad, do you think you can decide now?" I asked.

He emphatically shook his head no, which was no surprise.

I told him that he had to be discharged today and that I was going to go now and would check back with him in two hours to get his decision.

"Dad, have you had a chance to make up your mind yet?" I asked when I returned.

"No.", he mouthed, as he emphatically shook his head no. At this point he appeared to be really angry, which I understood.

I continued; "I know how difficult this must be for you, but you have to give up your bed here today and you will need to decide." He diverted his eyes from mine and looked away.

I reported back to the nursing staff that he could not or would not make a decision. It took a non-family member, the hospital social worker, to get him to agree to go to a nursing home. He was admitted late on December 11, 2008. And boy, was he ever pissed.

He didn't want to be there and it showed. I imagine that he was petrified of dying and was both scared and angry. He needed an outlet and it was easy for him to make me the target.

The admission procedure was long and rather impersonal as it all revolved around money and a lot of it. We got him situated into a double room with the agreement that he'd be transferred to a single room the very next day. He was very upset and would not respond to any of us. He would not even look as me.

The next day, many close family members came to visit him. He was conscious and seemed to be okay with them, but he was still very angry with me. I remember Stew calling me to see how things were going and when I went to answer the phone, my father shot me a very hostile look that ended up being the last look he ever gave me.

That night things went downhill fast and by the time we got to the facility Saturday morning, dad was unconscious and had been started on Methadone, which was now used to assist people transitioning to death.

Thank you, Dr. Kevorkian.

The head nurse helped us understand what was going on with my dad. She informed us that rather than cancer, he had shingles of the brain. She explained why he had a bloody pillowcase every morning. He had been trying to "pick" something on the outside of his scalp that was actually coming from the inside of his brain! She explained that the use of methadone would help him transition, painlessly. He was quickly going downhill because all the oxygen treatment had worn off and he was deteriorating at a fast pace. He was on his last stand. I knew from my nursing education and experience that once dad developed a fever he would not be with us for much longer and shared this with my mom and brother.

Mom and I stayed with him all that day with my oldest brother coming in and out as he had to care for his wife with Stage 5 Alzheimer's. Most of my relatives knew this was the end and were coming in all day to pay their last respects. At this point my dad did not yet have a fever but remained unconscious.

Then out of the blue, a strange thing happened to me around 5:00pm. I was feeling emotional as was my mother and we kind of got into a bit of a snit. I didn't realize it but I had begun to feel really, really, hot; so much so that I finally asked someone to take my temperature and low and behold, I had a fever of 102! How weird that here I was waiting for my dad's temperature to go up but instead mine did!

But prior to knowing about my own fever, I had climbed onto the bed with my dad essentially to say my goodbyes.

"Dad, I know you can hear me and I don't want you to be scared. We will make sure that mom is taken care of. It's okay for you to go now. I said, "It's time for you to join your mother and father. They are waiting for you!"

I laid next to him and told him that I loved him and that I forgave him.

My Dad now had a fever, so I left a few hours later to deal with my own.

Around 3am my fever broke and I woke up to soaking wet sheets.

I had been sleeping in my parent's bedroom because my Mom had moved both she and my dad out of it, afraid he might sleep walk and fall down the two stairs leading up to their bedroom. Talk about reverse roles. Dad had been sleeping in what used to be my bedroom while Mom was sleeping in my brother's old room (where we played Tickle-Tush) and I was sleeping in their bed!

I got up later that morning and told my Mom that I felt fine. She told me not to worry about going to the nursing home today; she would get a ride with my uncle. She suggested that I stay home and rest up. I don't know why, but I agreed and stayed home reading and watching TV. Mom returned home that evening to report that dad was still status quo; unconscious, with a fever, but alive. We had some soup and watched a bit of TV, before retiring to bed around 11pm. I read for about 20 minutes until I got sleepy and shut off the light.

I fell asleep almost immediately and felt Max, our deceased Maltese, on my chest licking my face. This comforted me at first, until I remembered that I was not in Palm Springs, the only place that Max had ever come to me to tell me that a spirit visitor was on its way! What was going on?

I instantly felt panic and turned from my backside to my right side when I felt the mattress shift the way that it does when someone is climbing into bed next to you. Then, I had the most unbelievable sensation between my legs! I felt an ache and at the same time a yearning to be touched; an energy that I have never felt before or since, but that was not all. The energy seemed to come out of my body and through me, rising up into of all things an open mouth, which I saw in this half awake, half asleep, dream state.

I know this sounds crazy and believe me, if someone described this scene to me, I would be wondering about his or her sanity, but this is exactly the way it went down. The only time in my life that I had experience with an open mouth was with Bubbie, the dog that we got after Max died. He and I used to play this game where he would open his mouth like he was going to bite me and I would put my whole fist in it and he would just playfully hold it there.

I can't explain why, but this is exactly what I did to this "energy" that came out of me. I stuck my hand in its mouth and at that exact moment, the phone rang. It was the nursing home saying that my dad had just passed away!

It was 11:40pm. I had only been asleep for 20 minutes.

Now, I know that this description and experience is pretty out of this world, but it is the truth and is exactly what happened!

I searched myself for a meaning in this experience and this is the only thing that makes sense to me:

I was in my parent's bed, in the same room where my sexual feelings got prematurely triggered all those years ago. I believe that those feelings were being returned to me 53 years later. I believe my dad came to apologize to me as well as to say goodbye. I say this because any other explanation would really blow my mind.

NEW YEARS EVE, 1976

In the November chapter, I relayed the incident where Vince broke my nose. We broke up that November day and I kept away from him for close to a year, even though he made a number of attempts to get back together with me.

About a year later I ran into one of Vince's brother at a bar in Buffalo. He was a really good guy and someone I liked and respected. He'd had a girlfriend the whole time Vince and I were dating but had recently broken up with her. And, if the truth be told, I had always had a secret crush on him. He was almost ten years older than I and really seemed to have it together.

Although his first name was Nick he had been given a funny nickname of Bump and to tell you the truth I had no idea why! When Bump and I ran into each other, we naturally hugged like we always did but this time held the hug for a bit longer than normal. We both had huge smiles on our faces and just enough alcohol in us to be silly and flirtatious.

He bought me a drink and we began to chat. I ended up telling him that I had always "liked" him. When he asked me what I meant I told him I "liked, liked" him and he admitted that he had always, "liked, liked me, too!" Well that was all it took. We went home together that night and began a one-year relationship, keeping it hidden from Vince.

It was hard because we both felt really guilty about going behind Vince's back. But the relationship with Vince was over and had ended sadly and badly but for me, but not for Vince. Every chance he had he would talk to this older brother about how much he wanted to get back with me. Bump, being the good brother that he was, would painfully listen and be supportive.

The holiday season was now upon us and Bump and I wanted to spend as much time together as we could. I had gotten very close to his family and would talk to their mom on occasion. It was no huge surprise when she asked me to join the family for Christmas dinner. But, what is *crazy* is that I said yes!

Bump was thrilled and through him, found out that Vince was coming as well. I was going to be between a rock and a hard place and the seating chart that his mom made was exactly that, difficult at best. To my left was Vince and to my right, Bump. That was nuts enough until Vince, who was so happy to see me, put his hand on my left knee, while Bump had hold of my right hand and was holding it under the table! So, imagine me, a right-handed person attempting to eat with my left hand! It was crazy!

I was literally frozen in my seat. It was exhilarating, scary, exciting, and nerve-wracking all at the same time. This could have been the end of this crazy situation but I think you know me very well by now and know that it was just the tip of the iceberg. Vince kept telling Bump how wonderful it was to see me and how much he wanted to get back together with me. To make matters worse, Vince told Bump that he wanted to invite me as his date to join him at an annual New Year's Eve Party that we had attended many times in the past.

Bump, who was also caught between that same rock and his own hard place, wanted to support his brother but also wanted his cake, me!

Later, he called me to tell me that Vince was going to ask me to this party and wondered what I wanted to do. Without missing a beat I told him that not only did I not want to go with Vince but that I wanted to spend NYE with him. He said that Vince had his heart set on me going and said he was okay with me accepting his invitation! I was shocked and gave him all the reasons why it wasn't a good idea. But he persisted and in a way insisted that I say yes. I finally gave in.

It was now New Year's Eve and Vince and I were going to go to go to the party as "friends." He came to pick me up (he now had his own car) complete with a bottle of champagne, a gift, and a corsage. He was so happy to be with me and it showed. The whole evening was so different from the past; he wasn't drunk or crude but instead was a total gentleman. He was so gentle with me; kind, loving, and sentimental. We really had a great time and when it came time for the Auld Lang Syne and the NYE kiss, well old habits die-hard and we were both quite passionate.

It was now time to go home and I was again staying at my parent's house as they were away skiing. We got back to their house around 3am and I tried to say goodnight to Vince but to no avail. He really wanted to stay with me. After numerous attempts to convince him to leave along with the late hour I succumbed and agreed to let him stay reminding him that we were friends and nothing more. Well, I'll bet you can guess how long that lasted. We kissed, we fondled and then the body took over and BAM, we were in bed with one another, caressing each other the way that star-crossed old lovers do, ending with a number of really intense orgasms for both of us!

Later that morning, after the champagne and pot had worn off, I woke up to realize what I had done. I was intensely guilt ridden and ashamed that I had not kept my word to myself and asked Vince to leave. He wanted to make plans to get together later that day to which I said no. I wanted to get to Bump's as fast as I could to make sure that we were still ok and to assuage my own guilt!

Vince left and I tried to reach Bump to no avail. I showered and dressed, with the plan to go to his house and apologize for my behavior and to make sure we were still ok. However, what I was met with was quite a different story. Remember this is way before cell phones and what I didn't know is that Vince had left my house and gone straight to Bump's house to tell him the "good" news.

By the time I got to Bump's a few hours later I was met with a door that was slammed in my face. Bump was beyond furious and called me a few nasty names that I'll leave to your imagination. I was hung-over, disappointed, hurt, and dumped, none of which felt very good on the first day of another New Year.

JANUARY

JANUARY

Up to this point, I've shared the most important stories of my life that helped shape me, month by month, year by year, into The Dancing Queen of Palm Springs but strangely, there are three events that all took place in January that actually impacted me more that any of the others. What's odd is that each event occurred within four days of the other again, from different years and different eras but still, just further examples of the synchronicity in my life.

JANUARY 20, 1961

January 20, 1961 is the day my youngest brother was born. We are 5 ½ years apart so I was four months into kindergarten on the day of his birth. I was never a clingy or needy child but instead, a very headstrong, independent, person. I don't actually remember the day he was born, but I do remember the day he was brought home from the hospital. He was very white and had shockingly bright red hair, almost orange, and a lot of it. Please don't think of Trump!

Having the role as the youngest or, the baby, of the family had allowed me to have more of my parent's attention, or so I thought; yet the minute that my brother came home I inherently knew that it was all over for me. I experienced sibling rivalry, which is typically common in children who are born a few years apart but not so common when they are 5 ½ years apart as we were. I know I tried to "help" my mother with his care, but I think that I was jealous of him and even at that young age tried to deal with negative feelings by over-doing what were perceived as nice things. It reminds me of the "Bad Seed" in a twisted sort of way!

As I got older, I actually became more threatened by the attention he was taking away from me and was kind of rough with him. I think I tried to shake him until my mother told me to stop it, I might hurt him. My mother said that I was mean to him and I realize now that I actually bullied him, as we got older. I *was* mean to him and I carried a lot of guilt about it for years until I came to appreciate that I was only acting out the same energy that existed in my home. My Dad had been a bully and I was recreating those feelings that surrounded me. I simply didn't have the intellect at that age to realize it.

I had two older siblings; a brother, who is seven years my senior and a sister, who is a little over five years older. They had one another for their pre-school years. My sister had three and a half years alone with my mother, while I had five years alone with her. So, although I had siblings, we were not at home together and were far enough apart in age that we weren't in school together either. It was as if I grew up as an only child and the baby of the family at the same time.

I had my mother's undivided attention, or so I would like to think, for those first 5 ½ years until my next brother came along. I lost my role as the baby the day he was born. I know that both of my parents loved me and that they did the best that they could. However, I think we all know now that most parents pass on what they themselves experienced in their own homes in various forms.

My mother was the second youngest of ten children and her mother adopted three other kids on top of that, so how much attention did she really receive? She lost her age placeholder when my aunt was born and perhaps she felt like I did, jealous! I now know that my mother had a big heart and wanted to be the perfect parent; so much so, that I think she forgot how to be a person. I clearly needed some very basic things from her that she was unable to give. Because my dad lost his own father at age 12 and became the head of his household, I'll bet he also lacked in the parenting department as well.

I believe it is also a telling sign that I don't have many childhood memories and the ones that I do have are mostly sad and uncomfortable ones. There was so much tension in our house that I was not a happy child but at the same time tried very hard to make people laugh. I most likely had the makings of a good actress! My mother always said that when I was good, I was very, very good, but when I was bad, well you can imagine. The photos taken of us all back then lack one thing, smiles. Seriously. We either look neutral, or sad, and often times I look depressed or mad. As this pre-dated photo shop these are unadulterated, real photos.

Sadly, my mother did not know how to teach us how to depend upon one another. This was especially noteworthy when it came to sisterhood and as a result my sister and I were never close even though we shared a room for the better part of 12 years! As a matter of fact we were competitive but didn't know it. My sister and youngest brother actually did become close. My oldest brother got married and moved out. I was left to get along with, and by myself. I will admit that it had both advantages and disadvantages but truth be told, I was very alone AND lonely in my own house.

JANUARY 22, 1965

This is the day that I got run over by a car! True story. I got run over by a station wagon in front of the ski chalet that my Dad and uncle had built in the early 60's. We were a family of skiers who lived in western New York State, one of the snowbelt capitals of the U.S., and I was on skis by the time I was four years old.

I was 10 ½ years old and my parents, as usual, were having a party that night. Earlier, around dinnertime, I got into a fight with my mother, but for the life of me I cannot tell you what we fought about. I only remember being very angry when I went out of the chalet to join my sister, cousins, and brothers to sled down the run in our front yard. We lived on a private, dead end road, which had very little traffic. We were able to jump, tummy first, onto our round "Flying Saucer" sleds and would fearlessly follow a bobsled-like path carved in the deep snow to the bottom of our driveway where our journey ended in the street.

We were so prepared that we had a "lookout" that called up to us as we stood on the top of run. We awaited their words "It's all clear!" to begin. It was no different for me that night and it was only when I was a few feet from the street that I heard my cousin scream: "Look out! There's a car coming!" I will never forget turning my head to the right from the sled to see two bright headlights coming my way. I must have passed out because the next thing I knew everything went black! I remember saying to myself; "I think I'm dead!" There was no light or sound and I could not move anything. Where was I and what was going on?

This was a private and unlit road. It was late January in the middle of a snowy winter at around 7:30 at night. Since we were out in the country, there were no city lights to illuminate the distant surroundings making it even darker. Our neighbor had been driving the station wagon and only later that night did we find out that he was drunk as well. I'm guessing that once he realized that there was a person on a sled, he swerved to the right to avoid hitting me. As his front tires zipped past me, my sled amazingly slid under his car and we, the car and I, hit the snow bank trapping me under the car, face down and still on the sled!

I was told that my cousins and siblings started screaming, which got the attention of my mom, aunt, and uncle, who were all in the house preparing for the party. They all ran outside when they heard the screams. My dad in the meantime had gone out to buy liquor and was not yet home.

I must have been unconscious for a bit but had now come to when I heard my mother's voice yelling; "Jillie, where are you?"

When I heard her voice, I was either on my way to Purgatory and got called back like in "O/A", the interesting Netflix original, or I was simply unconscious and trapped, but her voice brought me back to my horrifying reality. The only thing I wanted at that moment was my mother and as I yelled out to tell her that I was under the car, I vomited and then passed out in my own puke. Thank goodness I was still able to breathe and didn't drown in it.

Due to the darkness no one knew where I actually was. Did the car hit me and send me over the snow bank into the ravine on the other side? Or could it be that I was trapped under the car?

A bunch of the partygoers and my own Dad, who had just returned home, actually determined that I was under the car. I was told that 8 men lifted up this large station wagon to find me on my saucer. As soon as the freezing cold air hit my face, I was immediately conscious and crying out for my mother.

One of the partygoers was a nurse and was immediately Johnny on the Spot. I was on my stomach and still on the sled when she asked me not to move and if anything hurt.

"Yes," I said; "my back hurts!"

She didn't want me to change position thinking that I might have a spinal cord injury, but I didn't listen and turned myself over and reached out to my mother to be consoled. I think this is the first time in my life that I reached out to my mom for comfort. I was now on my back when the nurse asked me to wiggle my toes. It was at that moment that someone pointed out that the inner portion of my left boot was melted. We all looked down at my left leg and saw a melted boot with an intact ski pant leg beneath it. I remember feeling both lucky and confused. How could my boot be melted and my ski pant be ok? It seemed too perfect! And, guess what, it was! Underneath my pant leg there would be a third degree burn.

The skin had melted under the heat of the manifold, which had combined with the cold of the snow to form steam. It was this steam that had burned my skin. But, this was not as bad as it sounds because I was unconscious at that moment that it happened and I felt no pain, not then nor ever! I've gone on to have two plastic surgeries for the burn on my left leg and luckily have never had a problem with it in any way. The burn did not damage my muscle, and has never revealed itself to me as a problem over the last 52 years for which I am grateful. It is common for skin cancer to occur on burned skin but so far so good.

A few interesting things took place when I had my surgeries that I feel shaped my relationships to hospitals and to nursing itself and I'm sure influenced my decision to become a nurse. Frankly, the social worker field I had been interested in proved to be over-crowded at that time but it was my reaction to my mother when I came out of surgery that I think is the most important aspect of my decision to become a nurse later on.

I was having my second skin graft at Children's Hospital in Buffalo and was being wheeled back to my room after surgery. I felt really sick from the anesthetic and my leg and my buttock, the donor sight, really hurt. I hadn't quite come to when I saw my mother in the room and she was trying to get me to do something that I evidently didn't want to do but I can't recall exactly what anymore. I was ornery and feeling miserable and I snapped at her when she called me a brat. I will never forget how much I felt that I hated her in that moment. It felt as if I could not ever have one minute in my life that I wasn't perfect or cordial or could just be a kid, no less a kid in pain!

The nurse, who was in the room when this happened, saw my mom shoot me "that look" that said I was in serious trouble and somehow she and I connected over that look.

A few weeks later when I was released from the hospital I was upstairs in my bedroom. I had a full leg cast and was using my crutches to walk down the narrow stairway, making my way to the utility room where I heard the washing machine going. As I was walking through the kitchen getting closer to the utility room, I thought I heard a noise that sounded like crying. My mother was sitting on the utility room floor going through the laundry. She was holding some bloody clothes close to her chest and sobbing, something I had never seen before.

I called out to her and jolted her from her feelings. She must have been embarrassed because, she said, "Jillie, you scared me!" She looked uncomfortable and said, "Do you have any idea what you put me through?" I was not sure what she was talking about.

She continued, "Do you know what it was like for me?" She said, "I ran out of the house in my apron only to be told that it was you who got hit by a car! I was frantic and so scared. It was so dark out that no one could find you or your body. I thought I had lost you!" She said it was the scariest moment of her life.

It was at that exact moment that I thought to myself that there was something wrong with this picture. I was the one who got hit by the car. I was the one who had been under the car, scared that I was dead. I was the one who had gotten burned but yet she was focusing on her feelings and not mine! And honesty she never did!

I was a child but felt like I was taking care of her, not the other was around. As an adult I can only imagine what she felt and how hard it was for her, but I somehow knew even then that there was a role reversal going on. I think that it was at that moment that I knew I was going to have to take care of myself forever.

It would be many weeks later when my Dad told me what is was like for him to come driving up the hill to see a bunch of people and cars blocking the dark street. He said he got out of his car to see what was going on and asked one of the bystanders what was happening. It was so dark the person he asked did not recognize him said; "Oh, Guido Bianchi's daughter got hit by a car!"

I will never forget the look on his face because it was one that I rarely saw; it was the look of love and deep concern. My Dad wore his feelings of love tight to his chest but showed his disappointment and anger very easily. Today, I am grateful for that moment.

JANUARY 18, 1982

I was living in Chicago, Il. since July 4, 1980 with Vince. After Vince and the hostage situation, I had moved to my own place in Rogers Park and was working for the Institute of Psychiatry in the Peri-Natal Addiction Program. I had just left my job at the Visiting Nurse Association where I'd been working in a neighborhood that was then called the ghetto. I was back in therapy, this time with a male therapist, trying to make heads or tails of my life and was actually on my way home from a therapy session when the following life changing incident occurred.

It was a typical Chicago winter evening on this Monday night in January 1982. The temperature was freezing cold; there was snow on the ground, the wind was howling around the corners of buildings, and ice was beneath the snow making it very difficult to walk quickly.

I'd just gone to the grocery store to buy myself some food and was clutching my grocery bag close to the left side of my chest. Being street smart and savvy, or so I thought, I was carrying my keys in my right hand like a weapon and had my purse draped across the front of my body.

But it was cold out and the wind was blowing hard so I had my collar turned up over my ears and was for the first time in my life was wearing a hat! I say this because I grew up in Buffalo with winter being your enemy. Everyone there always wore a hat to protect their head and as a means of keeping the heat of their body constant.

Well, everyone but me.

My mother loved to tell me the story about how she would dress me in an onesie winter suit; put on my hat; pull the hood up over my head; wrap a scarf around my face all before sending me out to play. She claims the minute I got outside, I would unwrap the scarf, push back the hood, pull off the hat, and throw all of it on the ground before running off to play with my hair blowing in the wind!

So, it's significant that I not only owned a hat, but I also was wearing it on this memorable day. I think I was attempting to show myself that I *could* take care of myself because I'm pretty sure that my therapist must have made me question my ability to do so. Therefore the hat and the groceries symbolized my capability!

But, the hat shielded me from having peripheral vision and the upturned collar deadened the sounds around me. With the keys in one hand and the other hand circled around the groceries I was rendered defenseless. However, I didn't know that, yet.

I remember that I was not totally present in my immediate surroundings but instead was having an argument with my therapist in my head. I was not aware until my "guardian angel" pointed out that I was not alone on this dark, cold, street which ran along-side the El-train tracks; loud one minute as the train roared by and deadly silent the next. It was during the silence that I heard the footsteps.

They sounded loud and fast and felt like they were getting closer by the second. They seemed to be following me. I instantly felt the hairs on my neck stand up and felt sick to my stomach. But, I did not know how to trust those feelings or what to do with them so I kept walking.

However, I was definitely more alert and my mind immediately recalled a seminar that I had attended a few months earlier when I was working for the Visiting Nurse Association, which focused on safety and the values of being Street Smart. It was actually a fabulous in-service and I learned many valuable things, like what to do if you are being followed.

Rule #1 – Cross the Street

I found myself remembering this rule and did exactly that. But, at the same moment that I was crossing the street, I was actually challenging my inner voice, saying to myself; "Maybe this person lives on the other side of the street, too!" as they crossed the street along with me!

Rule #2 – If the person crosses the street run into the nearest business and start screaming at the top of your lungs

"Cool", I thought. I lived in a corner building that had a small grocery store across the street. Standing in front of my building contemplating if I should cross the street or just go into my building gave my assailant the seconds he needed to attack me.

He put his arm around my neck and pressed a small, cold, gun into the side of my throat. The second he grabbed me, I remember thinking, "Oh, one of my friends is behind me cause strangers don't touch you. But then I heard this voice that said, "Don't move!" and I didn't! I just knew I didn't want to die. I also knew I didn't want to see his face or look into his eyes, fearing that he would say, "Now that you've seen my face, I'm going to have to kill you!" No, that was not going to be the way I was going to die.

Somehow my feet moved and I went with him around the corner and into the first stairwell in the back of *my* own building. He forced me to give him my money, which was not much and he broke the light bulb overhead preventing us from seeing one another's faces. The only thing I know is that he was a black man and that is as much as I wanted to know!

He proceeded to order me to give him a hand job and then a blowjob. I had been hyperventilating from the minute he grabbed me which had rendered my hands and mouth useless as they had become paralyzed. Therefore, I was unable to get him off! It was then that he ordered me to turn around and he began to rape me from behind, not anally, but still from behind. He finally finished and told me to stay put for five minutes before coming out of the stairwell, which I did.

It's strange the things that run through your mind at a time like that. I was definitely having an out of body experience. It was like a dream. I knew what was happening to me, I knew it was really bad but I also felt like I was going to live to tell about it.

My thoughts immediately took me to my boyfriend, Vince.

You will recall that we met in Buffalo while I was in Nursing School and had broken up after he broke my nose. I had then moved to Atlanta, GA. to attend Emory, where I would get my B.S.N. in Nursing. He had been living in Chicago when he had been transferred with United Airlines. We had gotten back together once I graduated from Emory and I had agreed to move to Chicago to be with him. I had lived with him from July 4, 1980 until November 1980 when we broke up due to his drinking. I was living alone in Rogers Park were I was now getting raped. It was his alcoholic behavior that I found myself thinking about during the rape.

Vince would often times come home drunk and would become very sexually aggressive. He liked to dominate me; position me on my stomach and would force himself into me from behind. And I, sadly, let him do this.

It was only during this moment that I realized I had been letting someone rape me on a regular basis. It was a huge "Ah Ha!" moment taking place during this rape at gunpoint!

Lesson #1 - I have been raped many times

This would be the first of 4 lessons that I learned that night!!!

After waiting what I imagined to be five minutes, I crept up the stairwell in a definite state of shock. I numbly walked around the corner to the entrance of my building and walked up the stairs to my apartment where I knew I needed to call the police. (thinking back to the Street Smart Seminar, I remembered the policeman saying that if you have been raped, your body and all the fluids in it are evidence and under no uncertain terms should a person ever take a shower or bath or change their clothes.)

I picked up the phone and called the police and was numbly waiting for them in my apartment. The doorbell rang and in they came. They had sent a female cop to assist and I was very appreciative. I answered some of her preliminary questions when she told me that I would have go to the hospital to be examined. Knowing that this was standard procedure, I agreed to go and went to fetch my coat.

It was on my way to get my coat that the officer asked if I wanted to take a shower before we left. I'll never forget the thoughts and feelings that went through my head at the time. "Are you crazy", I screamed silently, "Won't that wash away the evidence?" Instead, I said nicely; "I think that I have the evidence in me and probably shouldn't do that." She quickly said that I was right and we were on our way.

Lesson #2- I do know what to do in the case of an emergency and am equipped with the answers. I can trust myself

Off we went to the hospital, my home away from home. As a nurse I'm extremely comfortable in a hospital setting, so this was no big deal for me. I answered the questions, anticipated the tests, and was eager to move this process forward. I was basically on automatic pilot. I was numb and in shock, but strangely, comfortable in my surroundings.

Once everything was done, I was ready and wanted to go home to take that shower and get on with my life. I asked if I could leave. I was told "no", I would have to talk to a counselor before I could be discharged. I reminded them that I was a psychiatric nurse and was in therapy but protocol was protocol, I would have to wait.

When I had first arrived, I'd been asked if there was anyone they could call for me and I said yes, and gave them my boyfriend's phone number. They told me that they had not yet been able to reach him at home (no cells phones back in those days) but had left him a message on his answering machine and were awaiting his call back.

I sat alone in my cold, small, ER room anxiously waiting the counselor's arrival. I wanted to get this over with and go home. Eventually there was a knock on the door and in came this tiny little person. She looked more frightened of me than I did of her. I was struck by her hesitancy and reluctance to make eye contact and flashed on myself as a nursing student. I had this sick feeling that I was her first rape case. Sure enough I was! It didn't take long before the roles were reversed and I was consoling her. She left crying, with me hugging her and telling *her* it would all be okay.

OMG, I thought, is this really happening? What is the lesson here? Am I the only person in the world who can take care of me?

Lesson #3: I can take care of myself better than anyone else

I was perplexed, freaked out, and numb, but totally present with all these lessons. It was now down to waiting for my boyfriend to come and get me. I remember thinking, and I'm sure praying, that he was coming to rescue me and would take care of me. Again, another theme in my life. Men and their role and/or their power over me. I was exhausted and was tired of taking care of myself!

The nurse finally came back into my room to say that my boyfriend had called back and was on his way.

These were the words I was longing to hear! "Finally", I thought to myself, "someone is coming to take care of me!" But, again, something much larger than me was in play. I was in this situation to be taught some very simple but painfully difficult lessons and there was still one more to come!

The man I was waiting for was a new boyfriend. He was a Social Worker who worked with me at the Institute of Psychiatry at Northwestern Memorial Hospital. We had only been intimate for a few months and things were a little rocky. It just so happens that he was also the first Jewish boyfriend I had ever had. I say this because as I was lying there waiting for him, I had a flash of some obscure piece of information that I had heard about certain sects of ethnic men. It had something to do with a belief system that considered women who had their periods or who had been raped were considered to be "dirty."

Don't ask me why, or where, or even how this came to me, but it did. I remember feeling totally panicked wondering if this was what was in store for me but kept telling myself that I was being ridiculous. How could someone think that I was responsible for my own rape? Or that I was dirty! I mean why would the woman be punished for something a man had done to her at gunpoint?

So, if I was to tell you that I might be intuitive and psychic, you might want to think that maybe it's true because my last lesson was the most painful of all.

I waited alone for about another 30 minutes when I heard his footsteps coming down the empty hallway. My bed was in the furthest corner of this chilly room. When he pushed open the door and stood in the doorway, he was as far from me as he could possibly be and still be in the same room. I took one look at his face and knew what he was going to say. I'm not sure if he even asked how I was, but I do remember what he said. "I would have been here sooner but I had to process my feelings!" He went on to say that he was sorry that I had been raped and hoped I would be okay. But, according to his beliefs, I was now considered unclean and he could no longer be with me! Did I understand?

Lesson #4 - I am intuitive and psychic

Because I had been intuitive, it lessened the blow but nevertheless it was incredibly horrific. I was too numb to fight back at the time and basically told him that I understood. I only knew that I wanted to go home and forget that this had ever happened, but knew I would not!

I know I slept that night and actually got up the next day and went to work. I told my supervisor what had happened and requested a week off to which he gladly agreed. I also called my best friend at the time and asked if I could stay with her in Atlanta. She of course said yes!

A few weeks later I got a call from the Chicago Police Department telling me that they had arrested a suspect for my rape case and asked me to come to the precinct for a line up. I was frankly shocked because I had only been able to tell them that my assailant was a black man who was about 5'9" to 5'11" and was most likely between 25-30 years old. That was all I allowed myself to see and remember on that fearful night. I immediately felt nervous and scared but put on my strong suit and got into a cab to go the precinct on my own.

I arrived at the station and was guided to the viewing room where I would get to see if my rapist was in the line up. Now let me just tell you that what you see on Law and Order is not what happens in real life, or at least not in Chicago in 1982. The room was of a normal size and it did have a very large window in it that was glass on my side and I was told a mirror on the other side. In the adjacent room stood 20 young black men! This is about 15 more than you typically see on TV. I was nervous but tried to be strong and yet it was still very eerie.

The policemen who were in the room with me were very nice and told me to take my time. There had been a number of rapes in my neighborhood and they had been bringing in all the victims one by one and hoped that they could finally nail this guy. There was no prejudice or inappropriate name-calling or bias that I was aware of and this was years after the Chicago 7 and years before Rodney King or OJ.

The first thing they asked me to do was to see if any of the men looked familiar. It was odd but I was drawn to one guy and told them so. They asked if I was sure and I said I really didn't know but it seemed so.

The policeman went on to explain what was going to happen next. He said that I was to walk up to the window and place my nose up to the glass. One by one the men in the line up would walk up to the window and put their nose up to the glass as well. I was to tell them if one of them stood out more than the others. This really freaked me out because even though there was a piece of glass between us these guys were going to be in my personal space, something that doesn't typically happen with strangers, especially possible rapists. I was definitely dreading this part.

They started with the first suspect and then one by one, the others approached me. It was awkward at first but really not too bad until the guy that I had first identified began to walk towards me. It was as if there was no glass between us. My body was certain that this was the man who had raped me at gunpoint earlier that year. I began to shake and sweat and I really felt like I was high. The knowing part of me was sure that this was him however when the police asked me if I could positively identify him as my assailant. I did not know how to trust myself because my mind kept saying to me; "What if I'm wrong and I falsely accuse someone and they go to jail? Could I live with myself?"

Sadly, the lessons that I had hoped I had learned during the rape were being challenged. I was still unable to trust myself and my inner voice, higher power, angels, guardians, protectors, source, or whatever name you would like to use for intuition.

The remaining guys came up to the glass but none of them elicited the bodily response I got from what I will now call "my assailant". They had him come up to me one more time and again, I had the same response to him that I had initially yet I was unable or unwilling to give them the answer that I knew they wanted.

As it turns out, the man I chose was the one that they had been trying to arrest for weeks, but not one of his victims could make a positive identification so they were forced to let him go! Today, I know that he was my rapist!

January 1982

The one thing I will never forget is telling myself that I refused to hate all men as a result of this experience.

My BFF at the time was Todd. Todd was gay and we did everything together. I moved out of my apartment in Rogers Park and moved downtown. I now lived about five blocks from him on one side and another five blocks on the other side to my job at Northwestern. Todd became my world and since we worked together and lived close to one another, we spent almost everyday together for the next four months. He was my closest advocate and turned me on to gay music and gay bars. We were inseparable and even began to look alike. He was quite preppy and I began to dress like he did but of course in a female version! He loved to travel and we were making plans to go on a train trip that summer. I was so excited to do something out of the ordinary and he was masterful at planning, like so many of my brilliant gay friends, that I am sure I felt taken care of for the first time in my life.

So it is probably not a huge surprise for me to tell you that I broke that cardinal rule between gay men and straight women and fell in love with him! Oh yes, its true!

I realized it one Friday evening in May and knew that I had no other choice but to tell him. We had a ritual on Friday nights where I would walk to his apartment, we would drink vodka and cranberry juice, smoke pot, play Earth, Wind and Fire albums, and get ready to go to the clubs after 11:00pm. I headed down to his place and knew that I would not be going out with him but instead would be baring my soul. I wanted to get it out of the way as soon as possible and wasted no time. He was most likely flattered but also knew the realities of the situation. I told him that I wanted to remain friends but knew that I needed to separate myself from him until my feelings simmered down.

I then very slowly and sadly walked back to my apartment.

I went to bed early that night and was sound asleep when my doorbell rang. I answered the house phone only to hear Todd's voice saying, "Let me in!" Stumbling towards the buzzer I hit it twice to make sure he had time to open the door of the building and then opened my door a crack and headed back to bed feeling totally confused and out of it. It took him about five minutes to get from the lobby to the ninth floor and my door.

He rushed in, closed and locked my door and began taking off his clothes. We had slept in the same bed many times after the clubs and always slept naked so in a way this as all familiar except that I had told him hours earlier that I was in love with him now and needed my space to deal with my feelings. I didn't understand what he was doing there. Well, that is until he got in bed with me and started kissing and fondling me and then started making love to me!

WOW! This was not in my game plan at all, but I was in, again, balls to the wall and had many orgasms that night! We continued this way for the next three years. We took our train trip that first summer and ended up with me being pregnant in July! (This was almost 16 years before Madonna's movie The Next Best Thing, where she becomes pregnant with her gay best friend, Rupert Everett, and has his baby!) Todd and I both knew that we were not equipped to be parents so I had an abortion that August. Todd and I are still best friends today and realize that we could be the parents of a 35 year-old child which would be pretty amazing. So, I have really been part of the gay community for a very, very long time!

Perhaps you can now understand a bit more about my life and the events in those Januarys that really shaped me, but it is this last event that took place on the eve of the Millennium that brought Stew and me together and it was Stew that brought me to Palm Springs and all of you.

Here's what happened......

.

NEW YEARS EVE/DAY – 2000

I was living in the Southwest with Matt and we had been running our folk art store for close to five years. Two gay men that I had met at the store had invited us to their New Year's Eve Party. They had recently moved from Idyllwild, CA., a place I'd never been but had heard about because of their world famous Jazz Festival. I had planned to attend this party with Matt. We had been planning this since way back in early December. He had obviously had a change of heart sometime earlier that evening.

I had been rushing around in the days preceding the party trying to find the perfect outfit. Matt was not a social person and in fact we'd never attended a party, movie, or social event together in the four-plus years we'd been living together so I had let myself get overly excited about this particular party.

Eating dinner together that night, I noticing that Matt had been rather standoffish and unusually quiet. I slipped off into our bedroom to try on my new outfit with different jewelry, shoes, and coats, hoping to choose the winning combination. I wanted to look my best on the eve of the new Millennium, the Big Y2K.

Around 9:00pm, as I wandered back out to the living room to see if Matt was ready, I found him with his head buried deep in the day's newspaper. I was flabbergasted and kind of pissed off. Had he forgotten that we were going to a party? I felt a chill in the room that was much colder than the weather outside. Feeling his coldness and my insecurity, I shakily suggested that he might want to think about taking a shower so we could leave for the party by 10:30.

My suggestion was met with an icy silence, forcing me to ask him again and this time from behind the paper I heard the words; "I'm not going!"

"What," I stammered?" And he again replied; "I said, I'm not going!"

I stood there; my jaw dropped to my chest, and tried to make sense of his answer but felt my stomach drop out of my body. I felt the blood rushing to my ears, my face turn hot and red. It seemed like ten minutes went by before I could muster up the strength to eek out the words; "Well, I AM!"

I remember my hands being freezing cold, while my face was red hot, barely holding back the tears as I walked down the hallway to my bathroom where I burst into tears in the shower. I was so hurt, so angry, so confused, and so outraged that I think I was truly in shock. Somehow, I managed to get dressed, walk back into the living room where I passive-aggressively said; "Happy New Year!" as I slammed the door to drive myself over to the party.

I had many thoughts on the drive over but the most significant was what I surprisingly said to myself out loud. "This is the straw that broke the camels back! I'm done! This is it!" I screamed to no one but myself as I shakily turned onto the street where my friends lived.

I should explain.

Matt and I met at my job almost five years earlier where I had been working for a woman who owned a clothing store in the hotel. At the time, I was married to Jack and was still living in Albuquerque. I have explained to you that Jack and I married after a one-year courtship that began with an unplanned pregnancy. I'm sad to admit this but I knew on my honeymoon that I had made a mistake yet being a loyal and hopeful person, I believed that I would grow to love Jack but, as you now know, I did not.

My boss had had her store in this hotel for over 35 years. She was getting ready to downsize and was looking for someone to rent half of her retail space. She asked each of her four employees to put out the word and curiously I was the one who found her a renter. I was given Matt's phone number and was told that he was interested in opening a Folk Art store. My boss was a very tough cookie and could be quite difficult to deal with, so I decided to call Matt myself. I wanted to give him a heads up as well determine their compatibility.

I placed a call to Matt on that January afternoon from my home in Albuquerque and left him a message. I was home alone when the phone rang an hour or so later and I answered. This was pre-caller ID and I only had to hear the "hello" of a very rich, sexy, east coast man to know there was something there that had me at "hello!" "Is this Jill?" he asked. "Yes", I said nervously. "This is Matt."

I shared the information about the store and my boss and the conversation quickly and naturally became spontaneous, chatty, and fun, with each of us sharing stories about our lives. How and why this happened was beyond my comprehension at the time, but the next thing I knew, thirty minutes had passed during which time Jack had gotten home from work.

I greeted him with a big smile and mouthed the word; "work" and kept talking. Jack was in the room while I talked to Matt during the second thirty minutes of the conversation. I said goodbye for now, as we had agreed we would meet the very next day for him to view the space. I saw that Jack was staring at me. He very pointedly and with a jealous tone asked, "Who *was* that?"

I remember thinking that he sounded jealous and was quite surprised because he was not the jealous type. I said, "I really don't know, we've never met" then went on to explain. He said to me, "You have energy with that person, I could feel it." I must admit right now that he was right! I was offended and dumbfounded at the time because I'm not the "me" that I am now and I denied his accusation. I told him he was wrong and that I really didn't know what he was talking about. I didn't know that energy transcends anything and everything. So, Jack if you ever end up reading this, I hope you can forgive me.

The next day, when Matt walked into the store I was blown away. I had butterflies in my stomach and was wearing a smile that wouldn't quit! We couldn't take our eyes off one another. We were instantly connected and the sexual attraction, magnetic. He looked like a super handsome version of the actor Gabriel Byrne, quite attractive and very sexy. This really was the type of man that I'd always been looking for.

During our hour-long conversation the night before, Matt had told me about his adventures and travels as an art collector. He had owned a gallery and a B & B in the northeast. He'd been traveling to eastern

Europe, and was now back from a big buying trip. He'd sold everything he had brought back from his first two trips and felt that he could successfully parlay that into a retail space.

My boss, Suz, was also smitten with Matt and they quickly came to make an arrangement that would go into effect the very next week. Out of the blue, she assigned me to be his assistant. (As I said to Jack above; Suz, if you're still alive and reading this account, I'd like to say "thank you" for making me his assistant, because it is this chain of events that eventually brought me to Palm Springs.)

I will never forget the feelings I had over the next two weeks because they were so intense and real as well as so powerfully sexual; physically and mentally. I actually fell head over heels in love with this man. It was as if we had existed as a couple many times before this meeting, in many lives and in many ways. I was all in, balls to the wall. I literally was orgasming numerous times a day, just being near him. I was inside of his eyes and he was inside of my head and body.

By Wednesday of the following week, I was weak in the knees and was beginning to feel like I was going to jump out of my skin. I finally mustered up the strength to tell him that I needed to talk to him and asked if he wanted to go out for a drink after work the next day. He said that he didn't drink but would be glad to go out for coffee. I remember thinking that 5:00pm on Friday could not come soon enough.

During those days I was staying overnight with friends in town to avoid the daily commute home Albuquerque, so I didn't have to see or think about Jack and focused all my attention on my meeting with Matt. I was getting ready to tell a basic stranger that I was in love with him but didn't know how or why it had happened! I was married, wasn't I? As we walked down the street to get our coffee, I was freaking out inside. I was nervous and excited and if I didn't know any better felt like I was really high!

We sat down after getting our coffees and I very frankly and directly said, "I know this is really bizarre but I think I am falling in love with you! And honestly, even if you don't feel the same way, I just had to tell you because if I didn't I was going to jump out of my skin!" I then took a big breath and said; "Am I alone in these feelings?" and he said, "No, you're not!"

I remember the blood rushing to my cheeks as I felt my stomach flip-flop and I looked deeply into his beautiful eyes. We sat like that for just a minute before he said; "But I thought you were happily married?" to which I responded, "So did I!"

He said, "Well, what are you going to do?"

"The only thing I can" I said; "I have to go home and tell my husband", which is exactly what I did.

The drive back to Albuquerque was like a blur. I couldn't wait to get home, but at the same time feared the encounter. I was feeling anxious and scared but knew I had to tell my truth as it was happening. I heard Jack's truck pull up and was waiting for him in the living room. He came in and took one look at me and asked what was wrong. He really was an intuitive guy, and a really good guy, but I was not in love with him. However, I did love him and certainly did not want to hurt him.

I have a very hard time not telling the truth, especially when it comes to the important things in life, and this was very, very, important. I knew that I needed to tell him the truth in a way that conveyed my feelings but also didn't destroy him in the process.

I must digress for moment here to share the process that led me to understand my feelings about Jack. A few weeks earlier I was to meet Jack at the movies. I arrived a few minutes early and was waiting for him outside the theater. Not being sure which direction he'd be coming from, I looked from right to left waiting for him to round one of the two corners. My distance vision isn't great so I had a hard time seeing who was who. As I stood there looking, I noticed a heavy-set guy at the corner walking towards me. I hate to admit it but I was very judgmental about this person in my mind and said to myself what low self esteem he must have based on his body language and walk. I was kind of disgusted by his looks.

I turned and looked in the opposite direction, knowing full well that guy wasn't my husband but couldn't see him coming in the other direction either. When I turned back, this "stranger" was now much closer and it was literally shocking for me to see that it wasn't a stranger at all but was, in fact, my husband. It was in that moment that I knew something was very wrong. I felt ashamed of myself, embarrassed, and guilty all at once. Sitting next to him in theater was painful and awkward. I didn't know what I was going to do, but I knew I had to do something! Maybe unconsciously Matt became my way out, but I was certainly not aware enough to figure it out just then.

So now, back on this pivotal day, suffice it to say that it was not a pretty conversation. I did not use Matt as the reason for my leaving because he was merely the catalyst. I tried so hard to be loving and accepting of whatever Jack's reaction was going to be, as well as caring, knowing full well that I was breaking his heart. I acknowledged that I was having strong feelings for someone else which is what made me realize that I was not committed to the marriage and knew that we needed to make a change.

It didn't take long before a very hurt and angry Jack said that he would take the weekend to decide what he wanted to do. He would give me his answer on Monday night. I said; "Okay, what ever you need to do!" and he left. I hate to say it but I was so grateful that he'd gone because the only thing I wanted to do was to go back up to Matt and run into the arms of my long- lost lover. And that's exactly what I did.

The 65-minute drive felt like a nanosecond and I could barely contain myself when I pulled into Matt's driveway. I was so hungry for his love! I'd been drug and alcohol free for over two years at this point and had only had sex without drugs or alcohol with two people since losing my virginity a few months before my 16th birthday. My first had been with Robert the Borderline guy and the second was Jack, who really wasn't my physical type but was a truly nice person.

Matt on the other hand was my physical type amongst other things so when we united there were fireworks. We literally fell into each other's arms in his kitchen, stripped one another and barely made it to the couch where we fell into one another's bodies. He had been a clergyman for most of his adult life so I will leave it to your imagination as to what the passion was like! I spent the entire weekend making love and felt like a million dollars!

Jack and I met that Monday night after work. After spending two solids days and nights in the bedroom with Matt I'm sure I was beaming from stem to stern. It was cut and dry for Jack, he wanted a divorce, the truck, the clothes I had bought him, and he wanted to finish the degree I was paying for with the money I made from my two jobs. I selfishly agreed to it all and six weeks later we were divorced.

Matt and I continued to work side-by-side during the day and side-by-side in bed most nights. He was leaving to go back to eastern Europe for a buying trip and shocked me when he suggested that I join him! OMG. A man whom I loved was inviting me to Europe, a place I had been dreaming about since I was a young girl.

I was so over-joyed. It was all so romantic. But I had to get time off from work so I lied to Suz, telling her that my grandmother had died. It was a wild time for me. While in the store, Matt and I pretended to be nothing but co-workers to one another but found reasons to meet in the hallways or the basement of the hotel to hug and kiss! I was having the time of my life on one hand, but found it difficult to tell people about Matt because I felt guilty about running from one man to another.

By the time Matt flew off to eastern Europe, I was divorced.

I couldn't wait to get to Europe and into the arms of my lover. I only prayed that Matt would be on the other side of Customs when I arrived in Vilnius that March of 1994. These were the days when making a long distance phone call, let alone one overseas, was both difficult and very costly. You had to get an operator to get you an overseas line and there were days when five or six hours would go by before you were connected. We may have only spoken twice over the three weeks prior to my departure. The second call being the night before I was to leave when we had a two-minute conversation before we got cut off. I had to have faith.

The flight over felt like it would never end. I was so nervous and so excited at the same time. We landed and I could immediately feel the shift in the air. I was in a foreign country and one that was very different from my life in the United States. No one smiled. Everyone was intense and in a hurry. There was no eye contact and the customs officers were chilly at best.

I was so relieved to see Matt waiting for me on the other side of customs. But somehow, he didn't seem to be relieved to see me! He was not the same man he had been in the southwest. He was not smiling and his eyes had an intensity to them that scared me to my core. It was as if he was a courier with a sign that said BIANCHI, hired to pick up a stranger from the airport. To this day I will never know what happened to him from the time he left to the time I arrived.

He barely looked me in the eyes or gave me a real hug before he quickly whisked me off to his freezing cold, but gorgeous vintage Citroen, one of my favorite cars. It's as if our story, which had the makings of the perfect love story, had been broken. I was devastated, hurt, sacred, sad, freaked-out, and angry all at the same time. What had I done? What was wrong? Had I misread this whole thing or made it up in my mind? What was I supposed to do? Should I stay or should I go?

We somehow got through the five-day stay with very little interpersonal conversation. I did what some people do in a situation like that. I became a student of the experience and took in everything I could. He taught me how to negotiate with the artists. We met with them in their modest dwellings deep in the countryside of Lithuania. It was all new and exciting on one hand and cold and impersonal on another.

I got used to using the large bills that were their money system; learned to make cash withdrawals from our credit cards in huge banks that were housed in cold, institutional looking buildings in cities throughout the country; met the customs officers whom we had to bribe in order to get our goods out of the country. I became accustomed to eating the food of the people; learned how to pack up large refrigerator boxes with the Folk Arts we bought using anything from old dishtowels, newspaper, or old letters as packing materials; praying that our delicate wooden sculptures would make the long 5,586 mile trip from Vilnius back to the Southwest.

At night we stayed in small hotels in tiny towns, many of which only had twin beds. Matt made no effort to push the beds together and I certainly wasn't assertive enough to suggest that we do so. There was no intimacy whatsoever. I think a normal, secure person would have insisted upon a conversation about what was happening, but I knew better than to rock the boat. My intuitive self knew how to deal with a person who was pushing me away. I had no power back in those days and remained silent but deadly.

I was unable to muster up the courage to ask him what was wrong. It was freezing outside and just as cold inside if you get my drift. It wasn't until he drove me back to the airport that I finally spoke up. I remember thinking that I couldn't leave without finding out what was wrong. We were in the airport parking lot when I shakily asked him if he was mad at me. He quickly said no, but offered no other explanation. I said that he seemed less than happy to see me but he said he had been.

This was a time in my life that I believed anyone else's feelings but my own. I told him that I was confused about how he felt about me and was more than shocked when he told that he thought it would be a good idea if I moved out of my house in Albuquerque and moved in with him! I couldn't believe my ears but then he handed me his house key and told me to make myself at home. I was literally blown away.

I flew home that night feeling like the happiest yet most confused woman in the world. It didn't take me long to pack up my entire house, find a tenant to pay my monthly mortgage, and move up to his house to start my new life. This included finding a gym near there where I would meet Stew, who eventually brought me to Palm Springs!

Matt and I lived together for the next four and half years, never recapturing those romantic, sexually uninhibited times that we had during the first six weeks of our relationship. Instead, we bought a house together and grew his little business into a small successful business that more than paid our bills. We made at least two buying trips a year. Often, I would travel to eastern Europe on my own to buy while he worked at the store, or vice versa. I learned so much from him and even learned a bit of the language as well. I am nothing if not loyal, so I stayed with him even though there was little to no intimacy ever again.

During this time, I had two girlfriends and each one of us was in a "strange" type of relationship with challenged intimacy issues at their core. My best friend, Gabs, and I were workout partners and focused on getting lean. We lifted weights together and also ran together. She had been an athlete most of her life and looked amazing. I, one the other hand, had always worked out but constantly struggled with my weight. I was both anorexic and bulimic and therefore ate away my feelings.

I was an exercise addict and used cardio as my new drug of choice. I was often times very depressed and was grateful to have Gabs and Susan, my other friend, as sounding boards and vice versa. I lived a very dull life, working seven days a week at my job, worked out five days a week at the gym, and saw a movie once a week with one of the two girls. I always had my music to fall back on and would dance by myself at home when Matt was at work.

After the third year of this non-intimate distance between us, I told Matt that I thought we needed to go see a therapist because we were not communicating. He told me that he didn't believe in therapy and would not go. I was so hurt and so angry but knew I needed help and told him that I was going alone.

I found myself a therapist. She and I worked very well together. I'd been in therapy before but it was the first time I had ever had a female therapist and found it very rewarding. One day she asked me to make a list of the ten most important qualities that I looked for in a man.

I very quickly made my list. She asked me to identify which of the qualities my current partner had. I can't tell you how shocked I was when I realized that Matt did not possess any of those qualities! Please understand that Matt had many wonderful qualities, just not the ones that I had delineated that I personally needed to be in a relationship with a man. I looked at her and said; " There is nothing else to say." I put the list in my wallet and left the session knowing what I needed to do next.

Now, back to Y2K.

It was some time after midnight on January 1, 2000 where I sat alone at this very loud, lively, and crowded New Year's Eve party. I was in a room with a small handful of people who, perhaps like me, lacked the self-confidence to be elsewhere in the house. We were all quietly watching CNN's New Years Eve around the world, glued to the TV making appropriate but mundane comments along the way while the rest of the partygoers were in other rooms of the house seemingly and naturally having an incredible time.

It had taken every bit of courage for me to attend this party alone. I was drug and alcohol free and I did not know any of the other guests except the hosts and had planned on being there with Matt, who was now home alone. Sitting there watching this incredible celebration around the world, seeing how life goes on, realizing that the dreaded part of Y2K was not going to occur and that a new chapter in all of our lives had begun must have given me the long overdue courage to do what I knew needed to be done, I had to break up with Matt.

I had to fight for myself and I had to be happy. It would be ten days later that I would have my first date with Stew. From that moment I would start attending circuit parties, gay cruises, become a personal trainer, and would begin a regimented workout program and eating plan that would not only change my body, my mind, and my spirit but would also lead me to my life as **The Dancing Queen of Palm Springs**!

EPILOGUE

Today, almost two decades later, I continue to "reign" in my publically acknowledged place as **The Dancing Queen of Palm Springs**. My soul and my psyche are far, far, away from that insecure person who shakily welcomed in the new millennium all those years ago.

That long-ago person, while formative and basic to the building blocks that are me, is really no longer. She has used each and every experience, the good the bad and the existentially significant, to craft, mold, and create the confident, caring, engaged, woman I am today. The rich and vibrant life I have now I build from hard knocks and hard work. I have no regrets. I have a deep and abiding gratitude to every person and experience I have been privileged to walk with on my own personal "Camino".

Over the years I have encountered and accumulated more friends and family here in the desert than any one person has a legitimate right to claim. I continue to live in the joy and companionship of the gay community that welcomed me so many years ago and look excitedly forward to the years to come, **Dancing** my way in the future.